EVERYDAY WISDOM

Time-Tested Principles
for Daily Living

Olu Ojeikere

Everyday Wisdom: Time-Tested Principles for Daily Life

Copyright ©2024 by Olu Ojeikere

All rights reserved.

First edition. November 10, 2024.

Published by Platform for Success Books

info@platformforsuccess.org

Dedication

This book is dedicated to all who seek and desire to apply wisdom in every area of their lives.

Special thanks go to all those who have, in numerous ways, Impacted wisdom into my life.

To my immediate family and siblings, thanks for being part of this journey of fulfilling my destiny.

I cannot forget to thank my bosom brother, Innocent Okonji, for his relentless encouragement and sacrifice in bringing this book to fruition.

Foreword

"There are several things that are important in life but of them all, wisdom is the principal.

There are several things that are crucial and necessary in life, but of them all wisdom is principal. Wisdom is a builder and an establisher. It has been proven over and over that success or failure in life is a matter of wisdom or the lack of it.

This book on daily practical wisdom by a very dynamic and serious-minded young man, Pastor Olu Ojeikere will add value to your wisdom life."

Dr. Festus Adeyeye D. Min. (Senior Pastor)

Abundant Life Christian Center, worldwide (ALCC)

Contents

The Genesis Principle

Nothing Grows Until It Is Started

"No matter how short or long your journey to your
accomplishment is, if you don't begin,
you can't get there."
— **Israelmore Ayivor.**

I t is not a mystery that the Bible, the oldest book with a detailed
account of God's character, principles, and works, begins with
the book of Genesis. "Genesis" means the origin or coming
into being of something.

Researchers, manufacturers, innovators, and developers from all
walks of life unanimously agree that to bring a conceived idea into
reality, one must begin with the end in mind. In other words, no
matter how skeletal or elementary the initial steps or product turn
out, the end product is always in view. You develop this end-

product or the advanced version of your idea, not immediately at the beginning but as you journey through.

This is the **principle of Growth** — that nothing is poised for Growth until it is started. God exemplified this principle when He embarked on the work of creation (Genesis 1:1-29). It is thus an inevitable process for any individual, family, organization, or society that craves Growth, new experiences, advancement, a better version of self, or other accomplishments.

Only living things grow. Therefore, once you bring an idea, dream, vision, or project into reality, it remains undeveloped and very much liable to being lost altogether.

BACKGROUND TO THE STORY

The creation story, as detailed in Genesis 1 and 2, reveals how the universe, the earth, humanity, and everything else came into existence. Interestingly, as the Scripture reveals, even though the earth was "formless and empty and darkness covered the deep waters" (Genesis 1:2), God went to work anyway.

The narrative reveals how God moved from one stage of the creation process to the other - creating light, separating the waters, calling forth dry land, plants, and trees, as well as the sun, moon, and stars, the birds, the sea creatures, and land animals. Finally, on the sixth day, God created humans, male and female, in His image and gave them dominion over the earth.

Quite notably, at the end of each of the six days that God spent on creation, He paused to examine the quality of what He had produced and saw that "it was good ."On the sixth and last day of creation, He did a general assessment of all He had made from the beginning to the end, "and he saw that it was very good!" (Genesis 1:31). In other words, God had progressively produced a masterpiece, despite the beginning looking so dark, dreary and daunting!

WISDOM NUGGETS

In this principle of Growth, God has laid a powerful template for us. Take, for example, the creation of mankind. A simple beginning, with the creation of just one man and one woman, has today multiplied to over eight billion humans on the earth. Similarly, the developments and advancements we see around the world today evolved through the growth process - through learning and improving on previous inventions and experiences.

So, how did things become what we now see and know? God BEGAN! Is it a mere coincidence that God had something big in mind (Acts 15:18) but chose to begin small and one step at a time? No. It is a principle He was setting forth for humankind — the principle of Growth - because everything that would come after would depend on it.

Again, as the omnipotent Being, God could have created the entire universe in one day. Still, He needed to establish the principle of Growth for humanity to show us that even He had to follow the process!

But the ultimate lesson here is that God began. Imagine that He never did! None of the marvels of life, the beauty of nature, or the remarkable advances in science and technology would have come into existence!

So, what is that idea, vision, project, or aspiration that you constantly dream of and imagine its completion? It is time to begin. As you do, bear the following in mind about the principle of Growth:

1. **Growth requires starting, even without a perfect starting point.** Someone rightly said that to begin is half the work because once you develop the courage to begin, it is easy to develop the courage to succeed. Sadly, most visions get miscarried because of the delay in birthing them. What causes this delay? Most often, it is the quest for perfection at the beginning — perfect concept, perfect timing, perfect number of resources, and perfect level of support.

   However, as God has shown us in the Genesis principle of Growth, the starting point does not require perfection. All the details do not necessarily have to be in place from the start. The determination to begin with the raw, infant idea is just enough.

   The first step of creation is the idea, concept, or vision in your heart. Usually, just as in the creation story, this idea may look unshaped, void, and dark, especially when you bother about all the details. However, the real light will not break forth if it remains just in your heart as an idea. That determined push to begin, no matter how small the outcome, is the catalyst that triggers the growth process.

2. **Growth requires work and determination.** In the journey to Growth, nothing is wished into existence. It is okay to daydream and visualize, but you must work the dream into reality. In other words, you can never see the fulfillment of your dream by continuing to dream; you must wake up to work out what you are seeing! As an Ancient Chinese proverb says, "Be not afraid of growing slowly; be afraid of only standing still."

We find this crucial attribute of Growth in the creation story. Despite His infinite power and majesty, the Almighty took time to work out everything we see, ensuring that each aspect turned out according to His master plan. He only rested when he had hit the targeted level of achievement (Genesis 2:2). God had to go through this detailed process to show us that even the best of visions would become worthless without the corresponding action. In fact, to show us that hard work is a fundamental part of the growth process, He did not stop at exemplifying it — He went on to institute it as a command. "Six days thou shalt work, but on the seventh day, thou shalt rest..." (Exodus 34:21, KJV).

Out of the seven days of the week, God mandated six for work. It is not just any kind of work that engages every element of our being. It will involve your time, thinking, visualizing, strategizing, speaking, getting your hands stained, writing, sweating, walking distances, learning, and lots more. This is why the Bible says, "Seest thou a man diligent in his business? he shall stand before kings; he shall not stand before mean men." (Proverbs 22:29, KJV).

Now, as you apply the elements of diligence to your work as outlined above, you have to be mindful of the necessity of staying consistent with them. This is where your determination is put to the test. It would help if you were determined to see the result or product you envisaged from the start. That is what motivates and fuels you to keep at your vision and to stay consistent, focused, and unwavering.

3. **Growth requires planning and takes time.** Understand that while Growth requires action, the action must be planned and strategic. What is discouraged is overthinking the starting plan till it leads to what is called "analysis paralysis ."Analysis paralysis is an inability to act due to overthinking a problem or overthinking the potential challenges associated with a course of action. As the creation story reveals, even though God did not allow the prevailing circumstances to hinder Him from starting, there is sufficient proof that He had a strategic plan of action that was carefully executed. This is seen not only in the order in which the creative process was done but also in the deliberate decision to handle each aspect one day at a time.

It was not a coincidence that God created light before creating plants and then creating animals before moving on to humans, who would not only need all the other things previously created but would also be expected to exercise dominion over them. Again, it was not a coincidence that God had to pause to assess His work output regularly; He needed to ensure that it conformed to His plan.

Also, as previously noted, God did not complete the creation process overnight; rather, it happened over the course of six days. Even at that, He had to give humans the mandate to continue maximizing all that He had done, which has continued to happen till the present moment. Growth, therefore, requires persistent and consistent effort over a sustained period of time.

4. **Growth requires discipline.** It must be stated, though sadly, that not everyone who begins well on the path of Growth eventually achieves their target. History is littered with tales of individuals who had great talents, ideas, visions, projects, products, and innovations but ended up in failure and sometimes in disgrace. A closer look at these tragic stories would reveal a common factor — lack of discipline.

Discipline is essential for Growth because it helps to provide a framework for you to achieve your goals. As Jim Rohn rightly says, "Discipline is the bridge between goals and accomplishment." In other words, discipline helps you to create the structure and consistency that is necessary to accomplish your desired outcomes. It helps you to stay focused on your objectives without getting sidetracked by distractions or setbacks.

Discipline helps you to decipher what is needful or needless in your growth process. It helps you to know what individuals, activities, and engagements that are helpful or destructive to your Growth. It also helps you to measure how much of your time, energy, and resources you devote to each aspect of the growth process.

Essentially, adhering to the etiquette of success is imperative for achieving growth results. Every field of endeavor has a set of codes of behavioral demands within the practice. It is, therefore, important that the ethics that stimulate growth patterns are known and respected.

Once you determine your "growth enablers," you must consistently stick to them. And, as you begin to see the indices of Growth, you must continue to review, make adjustments where needed, and continue to learn better ways to improve - whether it is putting in more time, adding more hands, making more investments, or cutting back in some areas — that is Growth!

5. **Growth requires a constant pursuit of excellence.** The pursuit of excellence is one of the most powerful drivers of Growth. As already indicated, perfection or all-round excellence may not be possible at the beginning; however, its pursuit is needed for continuous improvement, which results in continual Growth.

God repeatedly exemplified this vital growth factor in producing the creation of a masterpiece. He started from a place of emptiness and darkness but ensured that excellence was His watchword. That was why He kept examining His output daily. Again, even though He found that what He accomplished each day was "good," He did not relent until

He "looked over all he had made, and he saw that it was very good!" (Genesis 1:31). That is excellence!

Indeed, there can only be real Growth with the pursuit of all-round excellence. Whether in personal life, product quality, service delivery, staff behavior, customer satisfaction, delivery time, or the environment and ambiance of the business environment, excellence is the bedrock on which Growth thrives. So, begin every journey of Growth by striving for excellence.

God's excellent touch at creation is what keeps the cycle of life running to date. It is the key that has continued to unlock Growth and advancement in all spheres of human endeavor. The pursuit of excellence energizes and sets you apart on your journey to the zenith of Growth. It keeps you craving to improve more and more until you have carved out an unbeatable niche for yourself.

Bear in mind, though, that excellence is a lifelong journey, each stage of which may take time and effort. However, with constant practice, striving to exceed expectations, and applying all the other requirements of Growth mentioned earlier, you will attain the goal.

KEY TAKEAWAY

Overall, the growth principle from Genesis teaches us that even the grandest and most excellent of projects must begin with taking small steps, regardless of circumstances or the initial outcome. Without these simple but courageous steps that are subsequently improved upon, Growth never occurs, and the best of dreams becomes a mirage.

PERSONAL REVIEW

1. What is the most important lesson you have learned from the growth principle, and how will you apply it to your life?
2. Do you have any ideas, dreams, or visions that you have harbored for long without taking action?
3. What factors have kept you from acting on your idea, and how will you tackle them?

The Ruth Principle

Commitment Comes Before Upliftment

> "I believe life is constantly testing us for our level of commitment, and life's greatest rewards are reserved for those who demonstrate a never-ending commitment to act until they achieve."
> — **Tony Robbins.**

Commitment has been rightly described as the act of binding oneself to a course of action until the purpose is achieved. It is the state of being wholeheartedly dedicated to a person, cause, vision, or venture. This dedication invariably spurs a conscious decision to accomplish the objectives or obligations of the engagement despite the challenges or obstacles that may arise. This is the predominant message in the book of

Ruth, especially as seen in the relationship between the central character, Ruth, and Naomi, her mother-in-law.

Usually, when one is committed to a relationship, vision, goal, or course of action, there is a sense of personal responsibility and accountability to give one's best to it. This often involves a willingness to sacrifice one's time, resources, or personal comfort to achieve the expected outcome. The implication is that commitment is an indispensable trait for individuals, organizations, and societies in reaching set goals.

Sadly, it is becoming so rare to find true commitment in relationships, whether it is business or family. Even worse is the sharp decline in commitment to worthy ideals and ideas. Yet, in life, commitment is the pathway to many great experiences and rewards that are not usually visible from the beginning.

Ruth's story interestingly shows how committed one can be to a cause clearly filled with uncertainty yet holds a great ending. Many stories and events exemplify commitment in the Bible, but the story of Ruth stands out.

STORY BACKGROUND

Due to a famine in their homeland of Bethlehem, Elimelech and his wife, Naomi, along with their two sons, Mahlon and Chilion, migrated to the land of Moab. Not long after, Elimelech died, leaving Naomi a widow. As the sons grew, they married Moabite women, Ruth and Orpah. Sadly, both sons also died, leaving Naomi with just her two daughters-in-law (Ruth 1:1-5).

More time passed, and Naomi decided to return to Bethlehem. She requested her two faithful daughters-in-law to accept their fate, return to their homes, and begin their lives afresh. After much persuasion, Orpah chose to return. Still, Ruth, displaying uncommon loyalty and commitment, clung to Naomi and insisted on going with her (Ruth 1:14-18).

After they arrived at Naomi's homeland, Ruth continued to show commitment to her mother-in-law's welfare by gleaning in the fields for leftover grain. Fortunately, the fields were owned by Boaz, a wealthy landowner and relative of Naomi. Grace ultimately shone on Ruth when Boaz took notice of her and was pleased by her work ethic and commitment story (Ruth 2:1-11).

Fast-forward to Ruth's future. Boaz took a deep interest in her, after which tradition was observed, and the wealthy Boaz took Ruth as his wife. Ruth gave birth to a son named Obed, who became the grandfather of King David. Thus, Ruth's commitment not only paved the way for joy and restoration to Naomi's life but also launched Ruth herself into amazing prosperity and positioned her to be a significant figure in the lineage of the greatest king in Israel and, ultimately, the Messiah, Jesus Christ.

WISDOM NUGGETS

Uncertainty, or fear of the unknown, is one major reason people do not fully commit themselves or give up halfway, like Orpah. Yet, without defying all odds to make a firm commitment, there can be no meaningful progress or achievement. In other words, to succeed, you must commit - that is, give your whole being — to a worthy goal. Once there is a vision to achieve, the unwavering apparatus to engage as you saddle through the process is commitment. As Paul J. Meyer aptly puts it, "Productivity is never an accident. It is always the result of a commitment to excellence, intelligent planning, and focused effort."

Commitment can be to a cause with an outcome that is measurable in time — like obtaining a study degree, finishing a project, or learning a new skill. It can also be to an immeasurable lifetime cause with no preemptive result in view — such as a marriage relationship, growing a startup into a corporation, living out your faith, or being available for your child, family, or aging parents.

In whichever area of your life you need to improve your current commitment level, here are some basic truths you should know about this essential success factor, as exemplified by Ruth:

1. **Commitment requires choosing a worthy cause.** While commitment is a paramount recipe for success, it is not every goal or engagement that is worth committing to. Paulo Coelho, the Brazilian lyricist and novelist, once said of himself, "Freedom is not the absence of commitments, but the ability to choose - and commit myself to - what is best for me." In the case of Ruth, she made her commitment to follow Naomi based on what she knew about her, her people, and her God. Drawing from the years of interaction with Naomi and her family, she had come to understand the vast difference between the Moabites and the Israelites and between the Almighty God and the gods of Moab. Also, she was privy to the information that Naomi received that "the

LORD had blessed his people in Judah by giving them good crops again." (Ruth 1:6). Based on these factors, she chose the right path and stuck to it!

Learn to discern and decide your rightful path by looking inward and trusting in God, and then commit yourself to making it a success.

2. **Commitment requires sacrifice.** Commitment, as we have seen, involves binding oneself to a cause, a relationship, a goal, or a belief. This cannot happen without losing or letting go of certain entanglements, comforts, and even privileges. In other words, commitment must cost you something.

In the case of Ruth, she had to let go of her people and the comfort zone she had been used to from childhood so that she could be with Naomi. It was obvious that she could not hold on to Moab and Bethlehem at the same time, just as she could not choose to be with both her people and Naomi. She had to make a choice based on her priorities.

In the case of Jesus, he had to sacrifice some of His divinity, authority, and position so that He could be committed to saving mankind. His disciples, too, had to disengage from various entanglements to follow Him. In the same way, anyone pursuing a worthy goal or vision today must know that certain privileges, activities, habits, individuals, and places that may constitute a barrier, distraction, or limitation must be sacrificed for the main goal.

3. **Commitment requires loyalty and dedication.** Commitment implies a willingness to dedicate yourself wholeheartedly to the path you have chosen. This involves an investment of quality time, effort, emotional energy, and, indeed, your entire being toward achieving a particular goal. According to Ken Blanchard, "There's a difference between interest and commitment. When you're interested in doing something, you do it only when it's convenient. When you're committed to something, you accept no excuses - only results."

Ruth demonstrated this wholehearted loyalty and devotion when she famously told Naomi, "Don't ask me to leave you and turn back. Wherever you go, I will go; wherever you live, I will live. Your people will be my people, and your God will be my God. Wherever you die, I will die, and there I will be buried. May the LORD punish me severely if I allow anything but death to separate us!" (Ruth 1:16-17).

This is the intensity of commitment needed to succeed at any engagement. And if you check the record of all great and successful people in any endeavor, you will find this trait of unwavering loyalty and dedication. According to Henry Wadsworth Longfellow, "The heights by great men reached and kept were not attained by sudden flight, but they, while their companions slept, were toiling upward in the night."

4. **Commitment requires personal responsibility and perseverance.** Truly committed people have a deep sense of responsibility and accountability for their actions, decisions, and obligations. They understand that since they were the ones who chose to commit themselves, then they have the responsibility to see their commitment through. This naturally makes them persevere in the face of adversity. When obstacles arise, they are able to stay true to their goals and remain determined to achieve them. What made Thomas Edison commit himself to repeated attempts to invent the lightbulb was commitment. According to him, "I didn't fail 1,000 times. The light bulb was an invention with 1,000 steps."

Similarly, Ruth did not get to her place of exaltation overnight – her commitment reflected a high sense of personal responsibility and perseverance. For instance, when they got to Naomi's hometown, she took it upon herself to start earning a living as a lowly laborer so that she and Naomi would not have to depend on anyone (Ruth 2:1-3). She made herself an asset, not a liability because she accepted responsibility for her decision.

5. **Commitment requires a firm conviction or resolve.** Most of the previously mentioned components of commitment depend on this factor. Undying commitment to any cause must be with a firm resolve. You must believe in what you are doing, even if nobody else believes in it. The journey of commitment may not be void of uncertainties and

hardship, but it cannot be without a resolve to give what it requires to see it through.

Ruth demonstrated this resolve when she refused to be discouraged by Orpah's decision to turn back nor by Naomi's efforts to dissuade her. She was firmly convinced that going with Naomi to Bethlehem was what she needed to do, and she kept to her resolve. And, as we have seen, her commitment to Naomi ultimately brought her everlasting rewards, including a new family, a new home, and a key role in God's grand plan for humanity.

KEY TAKEAWAY

It would help if you were committed to a worthy cause to be uplifted by divine grace. Sometimes, you cannot have it all in black and white, especially the outcome. Yet, it might still be a journey to take. Remember, however, to make commitments only if you have an awareness of the true weight of involvement in what you are committing to.

PERSONAL REVIEW

1. What is the most important lesson you have learned from this principle of commitment?
2. In what areas of your life do you need to show greater commitment, and how do you intend to go about this?
3. Aside from Ruth, can you recall some other examples of people who demonstrated extraordinary commitment in the Bible and contemporary times, as well as the rewards they received?

The 1 Timothy Principle

Leadership Is Service

> "Do you wish to rise? Begin by descending.
> Do you plan a tower that will pierce the clouds?
> Lay first the foundation of humility."
> — **St. Augustine**

"Serving to lead" is certainly not the same thing as "leading to serve ."Leaders who adopt the "serving to lead" approach prioritize success in achieving targets. On the other hand, those who adopt the "leading to serve" approach prioritize the needs and wellbeing of their followers or team members. They focus on empowering others, developing their skills, and helping them to achieve their goals. They work to create a positive culture that supports collaboration, inclusivity, and mutual respect. This is the primary message in Paul's first epistle to Timothy.

Sadly, our generation has developed a different perspective on leadership and service. Wielding power and authority for self-gratification has become the norm instead of the proven approach of serving to lead. Apostle Paul's first letter to his spiritual son, Timothy, is an interesting lead in examining the principle of service in leadership.

STORY BACKGROUND

Apostle Paul had committed an entire ministry assignment to his protégé, Timothy, in Ephesus while he moved over to Macedonia. Timothy had this huge responsibility to oversee the church in Ephesus - championing, teaching, and defending the doctrines of the gospel of Jesus Christ, as charged and taught by Apostle Paul (1 Timothy 1:3-7).

The young missionary had been appointed to a holy office. It was expected to be found faithful in discharging the accompanying duties. The entire congregation of the church in Ephesus was going to answer to him - leaders, elders, men, women, widows, widowers, the young, children, and all. That was a lot of power! Paul, therefore, wrote to counsel him on the organization of the church based on the principle of service.

In the epistle, the older apostle addresses issues such as sound doctrine, the qualifications and roles of church leaders (elders and deacons), proper worship, the care of widows, and warnings against false teaching and improper behavior within the church. In all, the younger minister was expected to serve faithfully and be found blameless in the end (1 Timothy 6:20-21).

WISDOM NUGGETS

Imagine being given an office or a position with that much authority — having everything and everyone at your beck and call! What would be your approach to leadership? When you are elevated to leadership within an organization or a community, you are called to serve. To serve who? The people in your territory - your clients, citizens, customers, subordinates, organization, community, family (spouse, children) in any positively necessary way.

Suppose you are an executive or in some leading position. Do you see it as an arrival on a pedestal higher than the rest of humanity? Do you see yourself as some demigod who has begun to abuse privileges and derogate others? Or do you see it as an opportunity to enhance, guide, and support others to get the best out of themselves and reach their full potential?

Leadership is service. True service is selfless, result-oriented, and ultimately profitable. Everything sustainable and progressive must-have service behind it, not lording or usurping. Whether it is in a business, family, or marriage relationship or in achieving a dream, use every leadership role you find yourself in to serve and deliver values to people and causes.

To do this effectively, take note of the following about true leadership, as contained in 1 Timothy:

1. **Leadership is about humility and respect for others.** Leading to serve is only possible through a humble and respectful disposition. Through 1 Timothy, Apostle Paul emphasizes the need for leaders to approach their role with

humility and an awareness of their limitations. In chapter 1, for instance, Paul refers to himself as "the worst of sinners," and in chapter 6, he warns against the dangers of pride and self-importance.

Humility in leadership will naturally engender respect for others. In chapter 5, Paul specifically instructs Timothy, "Never speak harshly to an older man, but appeal to him respectfully as you would to your own father" (1 Timothy 5:1, NLT). He also instructs him to treat the older men in the community as fathers, the younger men as brothers, the older women as mothers, and the younger women as sisters in all purity. This emphasizes respect for others and encourages a sense of community.

2. **Leadership is about guiding others to follow the right path**. Leading to serve involves teaching and encouraging followers always to do the right thing. In 1 Timothy 4:6-16, for example, Paul instructs Timothy to teach sound doctrine. This involves guiding and educating others in the truth, providing encouragement, and empowering them to grow spiritually.

3. **Leadership is about caring for the wellbeing of others.** Leading to serve involves showing care and compassion, particularly toward the vulnerable. In 1 Timothy 5:3-16, Timothy is instructed to provide special care for widows. This highlights the importance of looking after those in need and providing support and care within the community.

4. **Leadership is about showing a good example**. Good leaders lead by example, displaying the qualities they expect in others. Paul, in his counsel to Timothy, emphasizes the importance of personal conduct and integrity. Indeed, throughout the epistle, the apostle urges leaders to exemplify the values they preach. He specifically tells Timothy, "Don't let anyone think less of you because you are young. Be an example to all believers in what you say, in the way you live, in your love, your faith, and your purity" (1 Timothy 4:12).

5. **Leadership is about shunning the abuse of power and privileges**. True leaders avoid misuse of their position for selfish gains or trampling on others' rights. 1 Timothy 6:6-11 emphasizes this. In verse 11, Timothy is particularly charged, "But you, Timothy, are a man of God; so run from all these evil things. Pursue righteousness and a godly life, along with faith, love, perseverance, and gentleness." This same admonition is a pillar of success for anyone in a leadership position today.

KEY TAKEAWAY

True leadership is not about dominating or manipulating others but being genuinely concerned about their progress and concerns. It is associated with virtues such as humility, service, caring for others, leading by example, and avoiding the abuse of power.

PERSONAL REVIEW

1. How has this principle of service in 1 Timothy helped your understanding of leadership?
2. In what ways will you be applying the attributes of "leading to serve" in your approach to leadership?
3. Can you identify any leader who exemplifies this "leading to serve" model from which you can learn?

The 2 Timothy Principle

Reliability Has No Substitute

> "Dependability is more important than talent...
> It makes no difference how much ability we possess
> if we are not responsible and dependable."
> **- Floy L. Bennett**

Reliability is the quality of being dependable, trustworthy, and consistent. When someone is described as reliable, it means others can depend on them to follow through on their commitments, meet deadlines, and fulfill their responsibilities. This trust positions such people to be entrusted with important tasks, receive promotions and build a positive reputation. It is for this reason that Paul's second letter to Timothy places a huge emphasis on this virtue.

Interestingly, reliability does not necessarily mean capability or competence, as one can be capable without being dependable or trustworthy. Since reliability is closely connected to personal integrity, people who possess this virtue are often in high demand. At the toughest moments of our lives, we seek reliable people to be our strength, confidants, and go-to people.

Yet, the quality of being reliable is fast becoming a scarce virtue. How discouraging it is to have capable fellows who could be more reliable. Such is the concern of Apostle Paul in 2 Timothy, as he urges Timothy not only to continue to prove reliable but also to recognize and appoint into leadership people who possess the same virtue.

STORY BACKGROUND

At the latter end of Apostle Paul's ministry and in the heat of his persecution experience, he lost many partners who had been with him through the mission journey to abandonment and neglect. He begins his second letter to Timothy by affirming the younger pastor's reliability in the cause of the ministry (2 Timothy 1:3-5).

He also mentions a few who proved reliable. He cites the example of Onesiphorus and his household, who, after the brethren in Asia had all abandoned him, stood by him without shame and supported him (2 Timothy 1:15-18). He particularly requests the company of Timothy and Mark to strengthen the ministry work that he and Luke are doing (2 Timothy 4:9-16). He further recalls persons who, despite being supposedly capable and competent, are failing in reliability.

Finally, he establishes that when all the unreliable fellows left him, the ever-reliable God Himself stood with him (2 Timothy 4:16-18)

WISDOM NUGGETS

In our current world, where almost every action or transaction is about selfish gratifications, how reliable are you? Can your employer, client, spouse, or contract partner go to sleep without fear you would circumvent a promise or an agreement?

Many skilled and competent people need to improve on keeping and holding up their end of agreements. Lack of reliability has become the bane of the success and progress of many relationships and organizations. Businesses cannot trust people; people cannot trust businesses either. Words are no bonds anymore. The government is failing on promises, marriages are failing on marital vows, and the failings go on and on.

Reliability is a great and learnable virtue. Suppose you are used to failing on agreements. In that case, you can begin with a decision to change and develop a trustworthy reputation. Here are a few things you should know about reliability, as established in 2 Timothy:

1. **Reliability springs from having sound principles**. As we think, so we are. Our external actions are a reflection of our internalized principles and perspectives. Therefore, to become a reliable person, you must develop a sound value system. Paul instructs Timothy to hold fast to sound doctrine and to guard the spiritual deposit entrusted to him (2 Timothy 1:13-14). In other words, the first and most important test of his reliability is his commitment to upholding and safeguarding the core teachings and beliefs of his Christian faith.

2. **Reliability is built by fulfilling one's responsibilities and obligations.** As you consistently fulfill your responsibilities and obligations, you steadily build a reputation of reliability that endears people to you and encourages them to trust and associate with you. Paul emphasizes this point when he urges Timothy to "do the work of an evangelist" and to fulfill his ministry (2 Timothy 4:5). The same calling is upon every individual today. There are too many broken hearts in the world. Therefore, make up your mind to become the reason why your family members love to be home. Be the reason why your organization is thriving. Be the reason why your staff choose to stay. Be the reason why society is a home for all.

3. **Reliability opens the door to higher opportunities and responsibilities**. Reliable people are often the first to be considered for sensitive positions, promotions, and higher remunerations. Paul shows how this works when he instructs Timothy to appoint reliable leaders who are competent to teach and who demonstrate a lifestyle in accordance with the Gospel message (2 Timothy 2:2, 2:24). The implication here is that reliability is a mobile advert. It can open opportunities and referrals, as well as attract useful relationships and networks!

4. **Reliability is best demonstrated in times of difficulty**. It is rightly said that a friend in need is a friend indeed. It is when things get tough and challenging that reliability is most tested and best demonstrated. To this end, throughout 2 Timothy, Paul highlights the necessity of enduring

hardships and trials while remaining faithful to sound doctrines and the work of the ministry. He specifically tells Timothy, "So never be ashamed to tell others about our Lord. And don't be ashamed of me, either, even though I'm in prison for him. With the strength God gives you, be ready to suffer with me for the sake of the Good News" (2 Timothy 1:8, NLT). He also commends those who choose not to abandon him and other believers in times of adversity.

KEY TAKEAWAY

A reliable person can always be counted upon. And if you choose to become one, the world will count on you. Therefore:

- Take every opportunity seriously.
- Value the feelings of others.
- Be conscious of leaving a positive footprint.
- Seek to ease others' worries deliberately.
- Be aware you can be the reason others are positive.
- Trust yourself enough to exceed expectations.

PERSONAL REVIEW

1. What is the most important lesson you have learned on reliability from 2 Timothy?
2. How would you be described based on the responsibilities committed to you? Reliable or unreliable?
3. In what ways are you going to improve your reliability rating henceforth?

The Ezra Principle

Trust The "God-Factor" As Your First and Only Option

> "Real satisfaction comes not in understanding
> God's motives, but in understanding His character,
> in trusting in His promises, and in leaning on Him
> and resting in Him as the Sovereign who knows
> what He is doing and does all things well."
> **- Joni Eareckson Tada**

You may be familiar with the phrase "the God-factor". It is what many people have come to trust in to conquer their human limitations. Trust is a strong belief in the truth or ability of someone or something. It is a powerful force that is very related to faith. Once a decision is focused on trust, all other look-alike options are considered not viable.

The story of Ezra, the priest (in the biblical book named after him), as he leads his people from Babylon back to Jerusalem, captures this principle. It is a story that highlights the importance of trusting in God in all aspects of life, the many ways in which this trust can be manifested, and the manifold blessings that come with this awesome disposition.

STORY BACKGROUND

The homeward journey between Babylon and Jerusalem would present Ezra and his fellow Jewish exiles with some grave dangers. King Artaxerxes of the Persian Empire had offered full military cover for the Jews as they journeyed. Still, Ezra had boasted in the strength of the Almighty God to save, and so they had set off.

With no military backup amid the reality of the danger they stood to face on their journey, their focus was set on God and God alone, having boasted their trust in His omnipotence. Then they fasted and inquired of God the right direction, ditching all other options except God's help. Guess what? God answered them and lived up to their trust and confidence in His ability to save them (Ezra 8:21-23).

WISDOM NUGGETS

The "God-factor" is often perceived by many as the last resort when all other options have failed. Whereas, for those who have wisdom to understand, it is the first and only resort. Too many times, people navigate life, viewing God's ability to help as a spare option. They are like, "I'll just do my stuff my way. If I crash and need God, then I will try Him." NO! You can get things right the first time. You can trust the God-factor from the start and trust in His guiding ability.

Set off that pursuit for any dream and desire in prayers, trusting in God's ability to lead and orchestrate things in your favor. Yes, you have the skills and are very knowledgeable. Still, no matter how skilled and knowledgeable you are, someday you will meet someone more skillful and knowledgeable than you are. Or it may even be someone less knowledgeable or skillful but with greater opportunities. Never keep God as your spare option.

The trust principle, as demonstrated throughout the book of Ezra, shows you just how to apply and benefit from the God-factor:

1. **Trust in God's faithfulness**. God is ever faithful to His promises. Whatever He says He will do concerning your life and destiny, He will surely do, regardless of the passage of time or the opinions of men. The book of Ezra is a powerful testimony to the faithfulness of God in keeping His words. Having previously promised to restore His people after their period of exile, God fulfilled it by stirring the heart of King Cyrus, who initially proclaimed their return to their homeland (Ezra 1:1-5).

2. **Trust in God's guidance.** Only God knows the end from the beginning, and only He has the secret of everything and everyone in his hands. Therefore, it is wisdom to seek and trust in His guidance in all matters. This is evident throughout the book of Ezra, with examples of individuals seeking God's guidance and direction in all aspects of life. Ezra himself prayed for guidance before embarking on the journey to Jerusalem (Ezra 8:21).

3. **Trust in God's protection.** Even the best of human defenses and security systems can fail. Only God can protect us from all forms of danger, whether physical or spiritual. Ezra and his people trusted in God's protection, and they later testified that "the gracious hand of our God protected us and saved us from enemies and bandits along the way. So we arrived safely in Jerusalem..." (Ezra 8:31-32).

4. **Trust in God's mercies.** As humans, we are prone to making mistakes, especially due to ignorance. However, as God has promised, He is ever ready to forgive once we admit our errors and demonstrate true repentance. Ezra led the people to do this and obtained divine mercy (Ezra 9).

5. **Trust in God's wisdom.** The greatest secret of having a happy and successful life is the application of God's wisdom. And the easiest way to access this wisdom is through the Holy Scriptures. Ezra understood this and led the people to renew their covenant with God and commit to following His commands. Ezra 7:9-10 reveals that "the gracious hand of his God was on him. This was because Ezra had determined to study and obey the Law of the LORD and to teach those decrees and regulations to the people of Israel."

KEY TAKEAWAY

Praying and trusting in God's ability for your good is your reverence of God. Do not keep that utmost factor as your spare. Make it paramount in your home, on your Job, and in everything else. Ultimately, in every venture, results will come from your encounters with people. The God factor will be responsible for your having the right information at the right time, encountering the right persons, and getting a favorable outcome, even when you ordinarily should stand no chance.

PERSONAL REVIEW

1. How do you currently position the God-factor in your life — first place or last resort?
2. In what ways can you demonstrate total trust in the God-factor?
3. What are some benefits of trusting the God factor, as revealed by the example of Ezra and his people?

The Job Principle

Reject The Poison of Negative Influence

> "Want to think big? Then get rid of the negative influences in your life."
> **~ Michael Port**

Influence is the power to affect the thoughts, actions, beliefs, or emotions of others. It is the capacity to make a difference in the lives of others, either positively or negatively.

Curiously, people are more prone to being influenced negatively than positively. This is probably due to the fact that the human brain is more susceptible to negative information than positive information. Moreover, people sometimes conform to negative influences in order to fit into a group or avoid conflict. The most common reason, however, is that people either do not have or really do not know what they believe.

The narrative of the biblical book of Job — especially the calamities that befell the main character, Job, as well as his encounters with his wife and his three friends - shows how he withstood a barrage of pressure to influence his thinking and behavior negatively. The book reveals the various attempts to make Job doubt his integrity and compromise his faith in God, as well as his resolve to resist them all.

STORY BACKGROUND

The Book of Job tells the story of a man named Job who was very wealthy and lived a comfortable and happy life with his large family. More importantly, Job is portrayed as a man who feared God. One day, God challenged Satan about Job's unwavering devotion, integrity, and reliability. Satan, in turn, scoffed that Job served God devoutly only because God had blessed him with massive wealth, health, and protection. He claimed that if God allowed him to take these blessings away, Job would ditch his devoutness and curse God (Job 1:1-12)

By God's permission, Satan touched Job's wealth and children, making him lose everything. Satan afflicted his health as well. Despite all, Job remains steadfast in his convictions and never turns against God (Job 1:13-22; 2:1-8). After that, negative influences came from Job's wife and his friends, forcing him to reconsider and compromise his relationship with God. The pressures came subtly in the form of counsel, advice, criticisms, and allegations. Yet, Job maintained his faith and integrity.

In the last chapter, God commended Job for not yielding to the wrong influences he faced and scolding his friends. After that, Job's losses are restored in double folds.

WISDOM NUGGETS

Everyone is a product of influence. Whether you are conscious of what influences you or not, you are a product of influence. However, you are safer in life by being aware of what you are allowing to shape you.

As previously established, people tend to be more negatively influenced because they lack a solid conviction about their own beliefs. Job was so trusted for what he believed that a proof contest ensued without his knowledge. And he lived up to God's boast about his devoutness.

Today, all kinds of influences are out there - positive, negative, relevant, and irrelevant. Be aware and be prepared. The story of Job gives some hints on this:

1. **Negative influence can come from unexpected sources**. One reason many easily succumb to negative influence is because it sometimes comes through close acquaintances and otherwise good people. In the case of Job, it came through his wife and friends. We must be vigilant so as not to be caught off-guard.

2. **The ultimate purpose of negative influence is to rob us of our faith and convictions.** Job's experience confirms this much, as the Bible says that despite the bombardments of negative influences that he faced, "Job

did not sin by blaming God." (Job 1:22). Much later, while rebuking Job's friends, God testifies of Job's unwavering conviction by saying, "You have not spoken accurately about me, as my servant Job has" (Job 42:7). God will give the same vote of confidence concerning you, if you would maintain your godly values, despite the pressures around you.

3. **Let your beliefs be based on firm, practical knowledge.** Negative influence cannot be defeated by mere feelings or head knowledge. One of the factors that helped Job to silence the negative suggestions and insinuations of those trying to influence him negatively was his sound knowledge of spiritual matters. This is apparent in the conversations he had with his wife and friends.

4. **Let God and His words be your final authority on all matters.** Despite all that Job heard, he ensured to engage God in meaningful conversations, in order to gain clarity and understanding.

5. **Be especially careful of pressures and suggestions in adverse situations.** Downtimes are very critical moments in our lives. All kinds of pity-party things come our way then; losers and helpers come as well, but our guards have to be alive the most during such times. Be aware and conscious of the following:

- Tough times do not stay forever, so imbibe calmness. Stay conscious of what you stand for and who you are.
- Refrain from scrambling for anything and everything that appears as a solution. Remember, both losers and helpers appear the same at critical times.

- Learn some endurance at tough times. It helps you buy some momentum for calmness. And you can make saner decisions in a stable mental state.

KEY TAKEAWAY

Knowing who you are is great. Knowing what you want is greater. However, guarding what shapes you is the greatest.

PERSONAL REVIEW

1. What do you know and believe in or about yourself, and what can you give or do for what you know and believe in?
2. How exposed are you to the needless influences out there?
3. Can you easily filter irrelevances when you are under pressure and feel like it is all caving in for you?

The Jonah Principle

Just Obey

> "The further you go in obedience, the more you
> see of God's plan. God doesn't often tell us the
> end from the beginning. He prefers to lead
> us on, step-by-step, in dependence upon Him."
> — **Iain Duguid**

The willingness to comply with an order or request - in submission to another's authority — is obedience. Our human self-will is sometimes very strong and overpowering when we allow it all access to control. God's willingness to guide and direct us rightly in our different quests is more often than not challenged to a standstill by this self-will.

God's guidance comes in the form of that still small voice, instructing and nudging us in an unpopular direction or that unpalatable counsel from a mentor or counselor or even your spouse; or that supposedly unfavorable situational sign and pointer; or sometimes through dreams, trances and the like.

When we fail to discern or obey this voice, we often find ourselves suffering needlessly. The story of Prophet Jonah in the biblical book of Jonah clearly depicts this.

STORY BACKGROUND

Prophet Jonah got a direct instruction from God to warn the people of Nineveh to repent of their wickedness or face impending judgment. Apparently, Jonah would rather God destroy Nineveh than seek their repentance because Nineveh was indeed a wicked land.

So, Jonah trashed the divine directive and ran. He took off to Joppa, and there boarded a ship to do his own will. As the ship sailed, however, a storm arose in the sea that threatened the travelers' safety and survival. After much worry and distress, Jonah was found to be the reason for the troubles and was thrown into the sea. The tempest ceased immediately afterward (Jonah 1:1-15).

However, for Jonah, his ordeal continued as a great fish swallowed him in the sea, as commanded by God. He remained in the belly of the fish for three days and three nights. Then, he sought the Lord's deliverance, repenting of his willful disobedience, and the fish, by God's command, vomited him on the shores of Nineveh. Thus, Jonah eventually found his way back to Nineveh to carry out God's original instruction (Jonah 1:17; 2:1-10; 3:1-10).

WISDOM NUGGETS

How many times do we end up in sour situations that we know for sure could have been averted if we had deciphered and adhered to simple instructions? I bet you can relate to this!

Obeying orders is not really easy, especially when they are not related to our routine job specifications or something that resonates with our self-will. When orders come from external sources on matters that are solely your personal life's quest or ambition, there is first this feeling of "Come on, I got this," or "It's my life, and I can run it," or "I know what's best for me."

Our self-will is usually the first responder in any matter requiring obedience to an order. We quickly consider what our best interest will be in the matter. Once we cannot figure out or place our self-interest, reclining is our next likely response. However, from the experience of Job, it is important to understand the following about obedience:

1. **God's will may not always align with our desires**. Unlike God, Jonah could not understand why the people of Nineveh should be given the chance to repent. He thus headed in the opposite direction, hoping to escape God's command. This shows that obeying God's will and plan for our lives requires us to put aside our own wants and desires and trust in Him.

2. **Disobedience often leads to negative consequences**. As Jonah's example reveals, these consequences sometimes affect not just the disobedient individual but also others

around them. This shows that obedience is not only for our own benefit but also for the benefit of those around us.

3. **Obedience requires us to trust God**. Just as Jonah eventually realized that God is the embodiment of wisdom, knowledge, and understanding, the wisest decision anyone can make is to trust in His plan. Even if we do not understand why we are being called to do something, we can trust that God is in control and that His plan is for our ultimate good.

4. **Obedience is the key to success and Growth.** Jonah's eventual repentance not only helped to avert the destruction of the people of Nineveh but also paved the way for him to be taught valuable life lessons by God.

5. **Obedience is the antidote to crisis**. All the troubles that Jonah and his fellow passengers experienced could have been easily prevented through obedience. Of course, obedience does not mean a shutdown of the brain, like you are some robot. However, identifying and obeying the right call — order, advice and counsel from a mentor, or even the unpopular inward nudges - can save you a whole lot of trouble. Imagine the troubles from credit card debts, living above your income, despising your spouse's opinions, breaking traffic rules, drug abuse and misuse, and so forth. The guides to avoiding these pitfalls are all available. Simply obeying can save us all the messes. We often neglect the guides, then go through the troubles and, like Jonah, come back to the right course.

KEY TAKEAWAY

If you are under authority, keep these in mind:

- Be conscious of your subordinate status and comport yourself accordingly. Realize that orders do not flow from the bottom but from the top.
- Have a willingness to learn and grow.
- Where you share a different view about an order, explore the most decent procedure to make a suggestion. But if not, stick to the status quo, obeying the order first.
- Recognize and respect hierarchy.
- Rebelling against authority is not always the best option. Quit, if you must, as a last resort.

PERSONAL REVIEW

1. What is the most important lesson you have learned from this principle of obedience?
2. How will you improve on your obedience to God Almighty?
3. How will you improve your obedience to constituted authorities?

The Ephesians Principle

Submission Is Sacred and Mutual

> "Since the marriage relationship is to reflect the relationship between Jesus Christ and His Church, it is imperative that biblical submission and love be practiced in all of its aspects between husband and wife."
> — **John Broger.**

S ubmission is the act of accepting or yielding to a superior force or the will or authority of another person. Interestingly, when Apostle Paul taught this subject in the biblical book of Ephesians, he placed specific emphasis on marriage. I am aware that this subject raises a lot of dust in marriage relationships today. Still, it is a sacred principle that we cannot avoid. Haha!

We shall, however, seek to point out the balance of truth that many tend to skip in this crucial principle.

SUBJECT BACKGROUND

Apostle Paul, having examined several subjects on Christian conduct and the need to focus on how Christ's work on the cross can supply us with grace to win, comes to the issue of submission.

In Ephesians 5:21, he begins with the need for believers to "submit one to another..." (horizontal or interpersonal), referring to it as the spiritually acceptable order. Still, he finishes that sentence with "in fear of God" (vertical, referring to the principle that governs and regulates every other form of submission). This means that God and God alone must be our number one consideration in all acts of submission.

The apostle urges believers to submit one to another but must ascribe it to God, the Supreme Being, to whom all humankind must submit. Quickly notice that in the next verse, Ephesians 5:22, he begins to address the spiritual leadership of the family, still on submission.

Have you ever wondered why scriptural teachings mostly put the Church and Christ (the Head of the Church) side by side in comparison with the marriage relationship (family)? Selah!

So, he says, "Wives, submit to your husbands, as to the Lord. For the husband is head of the wife, as Christ is head of the Church, and He is the Savior of the body. Therefore, just as the Church is subject to Christ, so let the wives be to their own husbands in everything" (Ephesians 5:22-24, NKJV). He immediately addresses the husbands, too, saying, "Husbands, love your wives, just as Christ also loved the church and gave Himself for her..." (Ephesians 5:25, NKJV)

WISDOM NUGGETS

The principle of submission is simple. Every submission is first towards God (through Christ, who is the Head of the Church). Whether you are submitting to your spouse or some authority, it is first in obedience to the Almighty — "as unto the Lord." Here are further details you must know about this principle, as highlighted in Ephesians 5:

1. **Submission is easier and better when both couples are in the Lord.** It is not okay for a man not to be "in the Lord" while a woman is living out the obedience of submitting to him. While that is never a yardstick for the woman's choice to submit, it might place the man on unsafe grounds. This is because God will honor the woman's act of obedience, and He will express the honor through the man (the head). So, if the man's position is a dishonor for what God honors, he is definitely not on safe grounds.

2. **Submission is reciprocal**. Note that the principle is the same for the husband's command as for the wife's. "Husbands, love your wives, just as Christ also loved the church and gave Himself for her...." (Ephesians 5:25, NKJV). The statement, "Christ...gave Himself for her", affirms that submission is reciprocal. While the Church

(woman) submits to reverence Christ (the husband), Christ gave Himself (submitted in redemptive terms) to save, protect and provide for the Church. Notice that neither command bears conditions as to why you should or not. It is unto the Lord vertically.

3. **Success in marriage lies in mutual submission.** Why was Apostle Paul admonishing families on spiritual leadership? The family is a prototype of the Church of Christ and bears a mandate of God's program on the earth. He used this principle to teach the wives and the husbands because it is difficult for both to keep their ends rightly "as unto the Lord" and at the same time allow Satan access into their home. Ultimately, therein lies the success of every marriage relationship as the Church of Christ is.

4. **Submission requires trust in God**. When we submit to one another in the home, we are ultimately trusting in God's sovereignty and wisdom. This is especially important when submitting to someone who does not seem to appreciate it, knowing that God will ultimately work all things together for our good (Romans 8:28).

5. **Submission is not a sign of weakness**. Contrary to what many assume, submission is not a sign of weakness but a display of strength and selflessness. It takes real grace to trust in God's plan and willingly submit to someone else, especially in the face of opposition or disagreement.

KEY TAKEAWAY

Marital success and fulfillment are not really dependent on money, children, exposure, and luxuries. While these tend to add to the overall joy and thrill, it is also true that many relationships without them are succeeding regardless. This means that the real determinant of marital success is mutual love and submission.

PERSONAL REVIEW

1. What is your view of biblical submission, and how have you been practicing it?
2. What benefits can couples derive from being mutually submissive?
3. What barriers hinder mutual submission, and how can you overcome them?

The James Principle

Words Are Creative Forces

> "The power of your words is enormous, and they also show the condition of your heart. Even your idle words will be accounted for in the Day of Judgment."
> **— John Broger**

Words are powerful. In fact, words are the primary known creative force of the universe. Our tongue is the organ and channel for releasing words. James, the writer of the biblical book of James, captures the principle of word usage - especially how our words shape our lives positively or negatively.

He observes that the tongue, though little, is responsible for the current state of our world, individually and collectively. So, what exactly is our tongue created for? What should we or should not use the tongue for?

James answers all that for us as we examine the subject.

SUBJECT BACKGROUND

James refers to a man who can control his tongue and speak the right words as a perfect man (James 3:2). He illustrates that bits are put in horses' mouths to keep them under control. Likewise, no matter how gigantic a ship's size is, it is driven and controlled by a small helm. So is the tiny tongue within our mouth. It is capable of doing so much, including the unthinkable. In fact, as James bluntly puts it, even the strongest and craftiest of beasts has proven to be tamable by human knowledge and skill. But the tongue remains an unstoppable cause of crisis for humankind (James 3:3-8)!

James further queries that knowing how much power our tongue wields, especially in producing both good and evil alike, should we then use our tongue to both bless God our Father and curse men? That is, should the same source be emitting blessings and curses? He concludes that this is an error that should not be. To emphasize how much of an aberration this is, he questions, "Does a spring of water bubble out with both fresh water and bitter water? Does a fig tree produce olives, or a grapevine produce figs? No, and you can't draw fresh water from a salty spring" (James 3:11-12).

WISDOM NUGGETS

Words! Words! Words!

Words are the key drivers of our existence. Every existence begins and ends with speaking words. Even where sounds cannot be voiced, words have their replica in signs.

We communicate by words.
We respond with words.
We react by words.

Take note of the following on the principle of words, according to James:

1. **Your words reveal the state of your heart and your eventual destination in life** (James 3:9-10). By the languages, dialects, and accents of people, it is often easy to tell where they are from and what their class is in society. This is the same with the words we speak generally. They reveal where we come from and where our lives are headed.

2. **Your words can build or break your relationships.** Harsh, critical, or deceitful words can damage your relationships, whereas gentle, truthful, and encouraging words can build and edify them.

3. **True blessings come from being consistent in your speech and conduct.** A spring of water does not produce fresh and bitter water at the same time. Moreover, regardless of our claims of spirituality or maturity, if our words do not match our claim, we make ourselves deceivers.

4. **Taming your tongue requires divine help and wisdom.** Since the tongue often proves untamable by mere human power, we must consciously seek divine wisdom, which is "first of all pure. It is also peace loving, gentle at all times, and willing to yield to others. It is full of mercy and the fruit of good deeds. It shows no favoritism and is always sincere" (James 3:17).

5. **Your tongue requires conscious control** (James 3:1-12). Knowing the enormous power that the tongue has, we must consciously exercise control over the words we speak before irreparable damage is done. While we need divine help, we must also be determined to be cautious with our words.

Here are a few things to be conscious of in exercising control over your tongue:

- Be empathic. People have secret struggles. They can speak up, seek help, and improve if only they find a concerned person who talks to them rightly and makes them believe.
- Do not be reactive—at least not all the time.
- Speak less, listen more.
- When things happen that get to your emotions, take a deep breath and allow some time to go by before you react or respond. It helps you approach the issue differently so you do not become a bitter water fountain.
- Try to smile more. Take things less critically seriously than they appear at that moment.
- Everything cannot revolve around your feelings. Seek to know why an outcome differs from what your expectations were.

KEY TAKEAWAY

Words create. Words destroy. Words inspire. Words demean. When you engage words in any given situation, which of these do you target? If you are in a position of authority, and you engage like a boss, a husband, a father, a wife, a mother, a teacher, or whatever position, whether in correcting, scolding, or arguing, ask yourself, am I a fountain of sweet or bitter water? The essence of every correction is to make things better, not to cause further destruction.

PERSONAL REVIEW

1. When you hear of a friend, an acquaintance, or a colleague's flaws and failures, how do you respond? Do you finish them off with the secret weaknesses that you know, or spare them those and find ways to help them overcome their challenges later?
2. Are you a bully by virtue of your advantage over others? Do you talk down on your spouse, children, or subordinates?
3. Do you even use the wrong words and talk down on yourself as a result of your weaknesses or past failures?

You can change all of that and learn to speak the right words.

The Judges Principle

Affirmations Produce Confirmations

> "Affirmations are our mental vitamins, providing the supplementary positive thoughts we need to balance the barrage of negative events and thoughts we experience daily."
> — **Tia Walker**

Affirmation is the act of declaring something to be true. It could also be a written or oral statement that confirms that something is true.

Everyone has a silent true opinion of their true self. However, either the wrong or right awareness may be louder. The louder is what drives us and determines our self-opinion, as in the biblical story of Gideon.

Positive affirmations are positive statements that can help you to challenge and overcome negative, self-sabotaging thoughts. Believing and repeating them to yourself often is the key.

STORY BACKGROUND

The Israelites had been under the bondage of the Midianites. However, as their cries ascended to God, He decided to bring them deliverance by the hands of a chosen Gideon. But Gideon had a wrong opinion of himself — he saw himself to be far less a warrior, let alone a deliverer.

Interestingly, God began the commissioning of Gideon for his assignment by affirming to him that he was a mighty man of valor and that He, the Almighty God, was with him. Gideon still did not seem to understand until further affirmations were made that led him to realize his true potential (Judges 6:11-17, KJV).

God further surprised Gideon by saying he was going to use a very unusual technique to defeat Israel's enemies. No weapons of war would be used but instruments of praise. How seemingly senseless! But that was exactly what God planned to do.

Knowing that Gideon remained fearful, God led him to hear a prophetic affirmation of Israel's imminent victory through the narration of a fellow's dream within the camp. This affirmation stirred courage in Gideon that victory was sure for the Israelites. He consequently embarked on his God-assigned mission and obtained a resounding victory in the quest (Judges 7:2-25; 8:1-21, KJV).

WISDOM NUGGETS

God's affirmations to Gideon — "The Lord is with you," "Thou mighty man of valor," and "Go in this thy might" - are proofs that no man can attain his full potential with a wrong opinion of himself. That is the principle. In our pursuits in life, we must master and engage the principle of affirmation. Today, we have the right and power to speak into our lives what is known as positive self-affirmation.

Here are some details about this principle, as highlighted in Gideon's story:

1. **There is great power in positive self-talk (affirmation).** When God first spoke to Gideon, he called him a mighty warrior, even though Gideon did not yet see himself that way. Through God's encouragement and his own positive self-talk, Gideon was able to step into his role as a leader and warrior.

   How sad that people talk down so much on themselves these days. Quit the negative first response to a huge task. Quit the "I can't," "I'm not good enough," "I'm not qualified," or "I have no resources." Embrace the "Yes, I can, "I will give it my best," and "I will find a way" approaches.

   This reminds me of the story of a little boy who held on to a small plant whose roots would not let him have an easy pull. He kept trying, and then he finally uprooted the plant. He announced in amazement, "The whole world had hold of it on the other side!" He applauded himself for a great feat. He defeated the world for all he cared!

2. **Positive affirmations are more easily obtained and activated when positive and supportive people surround you.** Positive people radiate positive vibes because they think, talk, and are active and positive. Associating with such people will always align your mentality with positivity. Gideon was able to find encouragement from his army of just 300 soldiers, who believed in his vision and leadership.

3. **Positive affirmations are best generated and strengthened by relying on God's words.** Gideon only found His true identity and capability by relying on God's declarations concerning Him. Therefore, regardless of what Satan or society may say about you, only the declarations of God concerning you (as found in the Scriptures and as personally revealed) should take root in your heart.

KEY TAKEAWAY

Affirmation does not often come from people these days, so you must self-engage this principle. Wake up every day affirming yourself concerning that task, challenge, or vision. Tell yourself you can and that you are going to give what it takes. Work at it. Where there is a will, there is a way. Remind yourself of this daily as you go.

PERSONAL REVIEW

1. Whose opinions do you rely on to shape your identity and self-esteem — God's or men's?
2. What kind of friends do you surround yourself with — courage-builders or confidence-destroyers?
3. What positive declarations are you daily making over yourself?

The Hebrews Principle

Faith Is the Master Key

> "Faith is to believe what we do not see,
> and the reward of this faith is to see
> what we believe."
> **— St. Augustine**

The dictionary defines faith as complete trust or confidence in someone or something. The biblical definition is, however, contained in Hebrews 11, which we will examine shortly.

So, faith is "complete" trust. As we explore the subject, we will see that anything short of complete is not faith at all. There is nothing commonplace about faith. It is nothing like just merely wishing for an outcome while eyeing a plan B or even a plan C; it is total trust.

The entire Bible is replete with teachings on the subject of faith, but the writer of Hebrews devotes an entire chapter of the book to capturing the acts of faith demonstrated by several Bible heroes and heroines through their life journeys. The summary of it all is in verse 6: "And it is impossible to please God without faith..." (Hebrews 11:6).

SUBJECT BACKGROUND

The Expositor's Study Bible, by Jimmy Swaggart, says, "Now faith is the substance (*the title deed*) of things hoped for (*A declaration of the action of faith*), the evidence of things not seen. (*Faith is not based upon the senses, which yield uncertainty, but rather on the Word of God*). For by it, the Elders obtained a good report (*God's approval*)" (Hebrews 11:1-2).

The writer summarizes these faith champions — Abel, Enoch, and Noah from Genesis, through Moses, down to Rahab and others - noting that, though their walks were all different, they all obtained God's approval through faith (Hebrews 11:4-31).

"And what shall I more say? For the time would fail me to tell of Gedeon, and of Barak, and of Samson, and of Jephthae; of David also, and Samuel, and of the prophets: Who through faith subdued kingdoms, wrought righteousness, obtained promises, stopped the mouths of lions, Quenched the violence of fire, escaped the edge of the sword, out of weakness were made strong, waxed valiant in fight, turned to flight the armies of the aliens. Women received their dead raised to life again: and others were tortured, not accepting deliverance; that they might obtain a better resurrection: And others had trial of cruel mocking and scourging's, yea, moreover of bonds and imprisonment: They were stoned, they were sawn asunder, were tempted, were slain with the sword: they wandered about in sheepskins and goatskins; being destitute, afflicted, tormented" (Hebrews 11:32-37, KJV).

WISDOM NUGGETS

A genuine Christian walk with God can never be short of anything but a complete trust in Him. In fact, faith, according to the Hebrews writer, is the only way we can please God. Hebrews 11 further highlights the essential truths we must know in practicing this principle:

1. **God's approval supersedes every other consideration**. Our primary consideration, as we pursue our dreams, aspirations, and expectations in life, must be that we get God's approval in the end. When we are pressed and pressured in situations, and we cannot seem to figure our way out, what is our quick resolve? Do we yield to the pressure of desperation to engage in approaches not approved by God?

   Desperate times provide the real test of our faith. As the full stories of the champions of faith in Hebrews 11 reveal, they all faced desperate times and common challenges like all men do. They had expectations for which they prayed, worked, and patiently waited for God's intervention. God's end-report of their walk was that He approved of them.

2. **Faith does not produce similar or instant results in all situations.**

   Consider the following:

   - Did the champions of faith face desperate times during their walk? Yes.

- While in faith, was there suffering? Yes.
- Was God's coming through automatic? Not all the time.
- Were there some quick results? Yes.
- Were there some delayed answers? Yes.
- Did they get everything black and white? Not all the time.
- Was God faithful still? Yes.
- Even with some dead without seeing the answers? Yes.

3. **Faith often requires patience and endurance.** Many of the individuals mentioned in Hebrews 11 had to wait a long time to see God's promises fulfilled. Yet, they remained faithful and patient in their waiting. As noted earlier, in the walk of faith, getting God's approval is more important than finding optional ways out of desperate times. Sadly, many believers are ignorant of this. Satan, therefore, sets his bait around this lack of knowledge and presses more on the challenge. Suddenly, time seems to tick faster, the desperation grows fiercer, and the believer begins to second guess his trust in God.

Trusting God in desperate times is the real trial of faith and the assured pathway to getting out of seemingly impossible situations. So, how much do you believe and trust? How long can you hold on, trusting? Many champions of faith died holding to their faith despite not seeing what they trusted God for all their days. God's eventual report about their faith, however, was that He was pleased with them.

KEY TAKEAWAY

Even if you have a supposed support structure you think you could bank on, making you feel you do not need the whole rigors of faith walk to address a seemingly simple challenge, still, learn to exercise and build up your faith. Trust completely in God for every outcome.

PERSONAL REVIEW

1. What is the most important lesson you have learned about the principle of faith?
2. Can you name 10 of the champions of faith mentioned in Hebrews 11 and what lesson each of their lives teaches you as a person?
3. In which area of your life do you need to exercise more faith?

The 1 John Principle

Loving God Requires Practical Demonstration

> "People who truly love God will willingly serve Him, excitedly tell others about Him, and long to worship Him."
> — **Richard Blackaby**

It is so easy to proclaim love for God verbally. But how does God want us to love Him? Even we, as humans, cannot live with mere verbal assurances of love for long. Similarly, God's opinion of mere verbal utterances of love is so low that we may be wasting our time and efforts.

John, the writer of the biblical book of 1 John, shines the spotlight on how God instructs us to love Him. It may be a tough call for humans, but the epistle tells us exactly how God chooses for us to love Him back.

SUBJECT BACKGROUND

John takes his time from the preceding chapters, teaching how God's love propelled Him to give up His Son, Jesus Christ, to redeem us, charging the body of believers to love one another as God commands (1 John 3:23).

He continues by showing that God is love and commands believers to live the Christian faith lovingly. God offering Christ to die was the height of expression of His nature of love. It became more interesting when John began to teach that love is best expressed in tangible forms, which was the reason God gave up Christ for our sins (1 John 4:7-10).

He nails it when he says God is invisible, but His love is in us by His Spirit. We can only speak of loving God because He first loved us and put that love in us. Then, he asks the big question: "If someone says, "I love God," but hates a fellow believer, that person is a liar; for if we don't love people we can see, how can we love God, whom we cannot see? And he has given us this command: Those who love God must also love their fellow believers" (1 John 4:20-21).

WISDOM NUGGETS

The instructions of God are simple and require simple obedience, but the ways of men are laden with selfish, deceptive complications. Our verbal, all-must-notice proclamation of "I love God" has been weighed on a scale by John the Beloved, and guess what? It failed God's approval!

God is love. When God loved us and expressed it by giving us Jesus Christ to die and redeem us from sin, He was showing us the principle of love. Man is not love and could not love. So, when God put His love in us by His Spirit (*"And this hope will not lead to disappointment. For we know how dearly God loves us, because he has given us the Holy Spirit to fill our hearts with his love"* – Romans 5:5, NLT), He was showing us the principle of loving Him. How? He did not deposit His love in us for fun. No! Every time we love others by His love, it is the love of God to them through us. And every time He can go through us to love, we prove we love Him. Loving others is God's approved access to show Him our love.

According to 1 John, the following is the nitty-gritty of true love:

1. **True love is practical and sacrificial**. If you love someone, you want to give up things for their comfort and well-being. You want to meet their needs and share your time and truth with them. Here is Christ's narration in Matthew 25:34-40:

2. *"Then the King will say to those on his right, 'Come, you who my Father blesses, inherit the Kingdom prepared for you from the creation of the world. For I was hungry, and you fed me. I was thirsty, and you gave me a drink. I was a stranger, and you invited me into your home. I was naked, and you gave me clothing. I was sick, and you cared for me. I was in prison, and you visited me.' "Then these righteous ones will reply, 'Lord, when did we ever see you hungry and feed you? Or thirsty and give you something to drink? Or a stranger and show you hospitality? Or naked and give you*

clothing? When did we ever see you sick or in prison and visit you?' "And the King will say, 'I tell you the truth, when you did it to one of the least of these, my brothers and sisters, you were doing it to me!'"

3. **True love is selfless and involves speaking the truth.** True love involves putting others' needs above our own, just as Christ put our needs above His by dying for us (1 John 3:16). But love is not just about being nice to others; it also involves speaking the truth in love, even if it is difficult (1 John 3:18).

4. **True love for God involves keeping His commandments.** True love for God involves keeping his commandments, and this results in a deepening of our relationship with him. (1 John 2:5-6). Christ Himself emphasized this earlier, saying: "If you love me, obey my commandments...Those who accept my commandments and obey them are the ones who love me. And because they love me, my Father will love them. And I will love them and reveal myself to each of them." (John 14:15-21).

KEY TAKEAWAY

Ultimately, this principle of love will hold true throughout the ages of humanity - that the way to prove our love for God is by yielding our lives as channels for God's love to reach humankind, by loving others — including strangers and haters. Of course, for haters, you keep them at bay but never serve hate for hate and never ignore any opportunity you have to show Christ-like love to them. This is the command of the Almighty God, as captured by John the Beloved.

PERSONAL REVIEW

1. What new understanding have you gained from this principle of love?
2. In what practical ways can you demonstrate true love to God?
3. In what practical ways can you show true love to humanity, including your haters?

The Esther Principle

Synergy Is the Soul of Lasting Success

> If you want to go fast, go alone;
> if you want to go far, go together".
> **- African Proverb**

The force of synergy has always produced more power for results than a single powerful force. It is the combination of two or more agents that produces a combined effect greater than the sum of their individual effects.

At a time when the entire Jewish race faced the most difficult period of their existence that could have resulted in their extermination, the trio of Mordecai, Esther, and the rest of the Jewish race residing in Shushan at the time showed the power of synergy. They commanded a prayer force strong enough not only miraculously to reverse an intended ethnic cleansing but also to cause the evil plot to backfire on their enemy.

STORY BACKGROUND

King Xerxes had just promoted one of his officers, Haman, to an exalted rank that required other junior officers to bow in reverence each time they saw him. News, however, got to him that Mordecai, the Jew, never joined this practice (based on his Jewish beliefs). Haman took the news personally and became hateful of the entire Jewish race. He craftily obtained authority from the king to eliminate all the Jews from the land of Shushan, providing a huge bounty for their execution (Esther 3:1-11).

As the news of the impending execution of the Jewish race broke in all the provinces, dread fell on the Jewish people. However, understanding the omnipotence of the Almighty, they turned to him for deliverance by mobilizing for a time of prayer and fasting in synergy. The plan was that Esther, the queen, would pray and fast from the palace while Mordecai would mobilize all the Jews to do the same in their different locations. On the third day, Esther approaches the king, though unofficial and, therefore, very risky (Esther 4:1-17).

That synergy stirred the spiritual force of reversal as Esther, the queen, found favor with the king. The Almighty God averted the ethnic cleansing of the Jewish race from Shushan, causing the entire plan to backfire on Haman.

WISDOM NUGGETS

Some things are achievable alone, but most great things are not. Some tasks and dreams can be delivered alone, but most cannot be accomplished alone. Learn the advantage and power of creating enough force through synergy. To do this, understand the timeless tenets of this principle as revealed in the book of Esther:

1. **There is strength to be harnessed in diversity**. Esther was a Jew, and Mordecai was her cousin and guardian, but they lived and worked in a foreign land. Esther was also a queen with access to the king, who had the power to help save the Jews. Other Jews in Shushan, too, had diverse strengths and abilities. Each individual brought their unique talents and resources to the table, and together, they were able to achieve their goal.

2. **Trust is essential for synergy to work**. Esther, Mordecai, and the rest of the Jews had to trust one another, as well as God Almighty, in order to successfully navigate the dangerous situation they found themselves in. They trusted that God was with them and would give them the wisdom and strength to succeed.

3. **Unity is the active ingredient of synergy**. As Amos 3:3 asks, "Can two people walk together without agreeing on the direction?" Esther and the Jews were able to save their race because they were working together toward a common goal.

KEY TAKEAWAY

No man is meant to be an island. So, identify your strengths and also recognize those who have other strengths that you lack. Find a mentor, get advisers, do internships, and volunteer with experts. Get a partnership where you need more than your knowledge or strength. Never be afraid to ask for support; do not be a loner when a little push from others can fire you up to greater heights!

PERSONAL REVIEW

1. Can you identify your personal strengths?
2. Can you identify areas where you need the support of others?
3. Can you identify people whose strengths can augment yours for greater results?

The Exodus Principle

A Vision Rightly Shared Is Rightly Actualized

> "Nobody can do everything well; so, learn how to delegate responsibility to other winners and then hold them accountable for their decisions." —
> **George Foreman**

I t is natural to conceive a vision or concept and want to protect it by keeping it to oneself while quietly finding ways to actualize the vision and then sound the achievement when it is done. However, the extent of progress might be mediocre, cumbersome, and burdensome.

From the book of Exodus, we examine the experience between Moses and his father-in-law, Jethro. We are especially interested in how his assignment as a judge over the Israelites was made lighter by a simple counsel.

STORY BACKGROUND

God had given the Israelites victory over Egypt and brought them out of captivity at the hands of Moses. Now Moses had to judge over Israel. He had sent his family back to Jethro, his father-in-law, due to the weight of his assignment over Israel. When Jethro visited the Israelites' camp, and Moses shared news of their victory and his office as a judge, Jethro watched him administer judgment from person to person, day after day (Exodus 18:1-13).

Deeply concerned for Moses' health and effectiveness, Jethro counseled him on the need to share his vision with other like-minded leaders and delegate some of his responsibilities to them. Jethro told him to introduce a simple, cell-group method of raising leaders trained to handle lesser matters while leaving only a few weightier ones to him. Good enough, Moses accepted the counsel, and things got much easier for him and everyone else (Exodus 18:14-27).

WISDOM NUGGETS

Burnout! Burnout! Burnout! Many visions and dreams die because the weight first kills the leader. Even the ones that manage to stay afloat can drain the life out of a leader who needs to learn how to share his vision or delegate responsibilities.

The principle of shared vision is premised on the idea that burdens and tasks can get lighter if shared with the right mind. Just one right counsel can drop the scale off your eyes and lighten the burden on your shoulders.

Here are vital lessons you can learn on this principle from the encounter between Jethro and Moses:

1. **A shared vision ensures the pursuit of a common goal.** Jethro advised Moses to establish a clear vision and purpose for the leadership structure. This highlights the importance of a shared vision and purpose within any organization or community to achieve common goals.

2. **A shared vision ensures proper delegation and prevents burnout**. Delegation allowed Moses to share his workload and avoid burnout. This teaches the significance of empowering others by delegating tasks and responsibilities, fostering a sense of ownership and accountability.

3. **Shared vision enhances effectiveness and efficiency.** Jethro's advice helped Moses to streamline decision-making processes in the Israelites' camp. Empowering your team members to handle specific matters will pave the way for quicker and more effective decision-making, ensuring that important issues are addressed promptly.

KEY TAKEAWAY

Jethro showed Moses the power of cell groups. Someone can help you lighten the burden of that supposedly impossible target if you can share your struggle and get good advice. It could be a marital, business, relationship, emotional, or spiritual struggle. No matter how big a city is, you could fly in a plane to a height where your thumb alone covers it from sight. That means it tends to look much smaller to you. That is how a shared vision can make a big task, dream, or problem look.

PERSONAL REVIEW

1. What is the most important lesson you have learned from the principle of shared vision?
2. Are there areas of your life in which you are bearing a burden that could be easily shared?
3. Identify other key people in history who have succeeded better by sharing their vision with others.

The 2 Kings Principle

Go the Extra Mile to Be Extraordinary

> "One of the most important principles of success is developing the habit of going the extra mile."
> ~ **Napoleon Hill**

The inability to go the extra mile on a cause might be the one single reason why many decisions and commitments die or fail. Going the extra mile means putting in additional effort or going beyond what is expected or required in a particular situation. It involves showing dedication, commitment, and going above and beyond the call of duty to achieve a goal or provide exceptional service.

There is something about that extra persevering push to exceed expectations. The encounter between King Joash (also known as

Jehoash) and Prophet Elisha, as found in 2 Kings 13:14-19, perfectly illustrates this!

STORY BACKGROUND

Shortly before Prophet Elisha's death, the then king of Israel, Joash, visited the prophet to inquire about God's deliverance for Israel from the oppression of the Syrians (called "Arameans" in some Bible versions). Elisha took him through a prophetic exercise of shooting an arrow through a window eastward to confirm God's deliverance.

Elisha then asked the king, in a second exercise, to strike the arrow on the ground, perhaps to seal the extent of victory. King Joash struck just three times and stopped. This disappointed Elisha, and he queried the king's decision to stop after just three strikes. He then said the victory would have been total if the king had persisted up to five or six strikes. After that, Elisha died, and Israel suffered more oppression from the Syrians (2 Kings 13:14-22).

WISDOM NUGGETS

There is a solution to every challenge as we focus on the techniques or knowledge we have about navigating our way out. However, too many times, we give up too easily. Here is how to overcome this tendency, as revealed by the principle of going the extra mile in Elisha and King Joash's story:

1. **Understand that there can be no true or lasting success without going the extra mile.** Joash only struck the ground three times when he could have done more.

When we go the extra mile, we need to keep pressing forward even when it gets difficult. The pains and the failures are all part of the journey. But that persisting spirit that makes you want to put in a little more time, learn a little more of that skill, give it a little more energy, tweak your approach a little more, stay the cause some more through painful, stressful times, or to see a counselor over that relationship issues, or to talk things over and make an adjustment - that is the extra mile.

2. **Going the extra mile involves seeing a process through to completion.** Joash's limited action reflects the danger of failing to follow through or complete a task to its fullest extent. Going the extra mile often means seeing tasks through to completion, even when it requires more time and effort than initially expected.

3. **Going the extra mile inspires followers and team members to do the same.** Joash needed to set a better example as a leader. His limited success serves as a reminder of the responsibility to lead with diligence and a commitment to achieving set goals. Leaders who go the extra mile inspire dedication and drive within their teams or followers.

KEY TAKEAWAY

Quit quitting too easily. The great achievements you admire in others take a lot of work. You just only have to hear the stories of those journeys to know why you should not quit. Your dreams will demand you stay the cause through pain and hardship, doing what you believe in over and over again until you eventually weather the storm for victory.

PERSONAL REVIEW

1. Would you describe yourself as someone who loves to go the extra mile, or are you like King Joash?
2. In which areas of your life should you be doing more to go the extra mile?
3. In what ways are you resolving to do better in going the extra mile?

The Mark Principle

Everyone Needs Some Support

> "You can't achieve anything entirely by yourself. There's a support system that is a basic requirement of human existence. To be happy and successful on earth, you just have to have people that you rely on."
> **- Michael Schur**

Everyone needs support or, at least, has required it at some point in their journey. As George Adams rightly observed, "There is no such thing as a 'self-made man.' We are made up of thousands of others. Everyone who has ever done a kind deed for us or spoken one Word of encouragement to us has entered into the makeup of our character and of our thoughts, as well as our success."

However, getting support becomes even more interesting and uplifting when the beneficiary almost totally cannot do anything about the situation. It is a great blessing. The story of the paralytic man and his four friends in the biblical book of Mark hits home.

STORY BACKGROUND

Four friends got news that Jesus was in town and ministering at a venue. Everywhere was jam-packed when they arrived with their friend who was paralyzed—no access through the door or the windows.

Determined that their paralyzed friend, whom they had brought in a mat, should get healing from Jesus that day, they found their way through the roof of the house where Jesus was teaching. They simply pulled off a section of the roof and let their sick friend down before Jesus.

Jesus was impressed by the faith of the four friends, and He healed their sick friend immediately (Mark 2:1-5).

WISDOM NUGGETS

It is good to get support from people when you are in need. But, here, let us look at offering the support. To what extent can you go to offer support to a needy person? If you were going to help someone get access to a place and the doors were locked, would you break it open? Those four guys removed the roof of a house they did not own. Haha!

Notice that Jesus commended their faith and, by it, healed their friend. This means that our effort and sacrifice in helping and supporting people is of great value before God. Here are more lessons on this principle from the story of the paralytic man and his friends:

1. **To offer meaningful support, you must take action**. Beyond wishing others well, it is necessary to take actions that can positively impact their lives. The four friends did not just pray for the paralytic man; they acted and brought him to Jesus.

2. **To offer support, you should be willing to make sacrifices**. The four friends went to great lengths to help the paralytic man, including going through the stress of removing the roof of the house to get him to Jesus. When offering support, it is important to be willing to make sacrifices and put in the effort to help others.

3. **To offer support, you need to be persistent.** The friends were willing to remove the roof of the house and lower their friend down to Jesus because they were determined to get him help. They did not let obstacles get in their way. When supporting someone, it is important to be persistent and not give up easily.

KEY TAKEAWAY

Our support for people can buy them hope. It can lift their spirit to continue in life, achieve their dreams, and build momentum. Do not hold back support from people; you might be the only reason they will live, survive, or even succeed.

PERSONAL REVIEW

1. How far can you sacrifice to help a friend or even a stranger?
2. Can you compile a list of people around you that currently need some support?
3. What efforts will you make to alleviate the burdens of the people you listed above?

Every Good Turn Deserves a Better One (Reciprocity)

> "Life cannot subsist in society but by reciprocal concessions."
> — **Samuel Johnson**

Reciprocity is the act of paying back a kindness or a favor. It is encouraged to keep records of kind acts but never records of evil because that is unhealthy, both spiritually and physically. Kindness is sweet when received, but it is sweeter when initiated or reciprocated (Acts 20:38).

The story of King David and Jonathan's son Mephibosheth (2 Samuel 9:1-13) is one with great lessons on the subject of reciprocity. It shows the importance of treating others with fairness and justice while demonstrating true kindness and compassion.

STORY BACKGROUND

David had become king in Israel after the death of his bosom friend, Jonathan, and King Saul, Jonathan's Father. Remembering the house of King Saul and the kindness Jonathan showed him during his turbulent days at the palace, he asked if there was any left of the family to whom he could show kindness.

His servants told him about the surviving son of Jonathan, Mephibosheth, who was lame. David sent for Mephibosheth, and he was brought to the palace. It was, for the young cripple, a day of destiny. Mephibosheth would then reside in King David's palace, eating at the same table as the king. Also, his farmlands, from tilling to cultivation till harvest, would be tended by the late King Saul's steward and his entire family of 15 sons and 20 servants.

How sweetly can one's fortune change simply by the reciprocation of kindness from a grateful soul like King David?

WISDOM NUGGETS

The sacrifice that pleases God is kindness reciprocated, not evil repaid. God planned it so. Acts of kindness are the acts of God. When you show kindness or reciprocate one, you replicate the nature of God and keep the chain unbroken.

The kindness you show today can be what triggers a breakthrough for you tomorrow. It can speak for your family anytime, anywhere, when you least expect it. Indeed, the reward for kindness does not necessarily have to come from the same beneficiary or in the same manner in which it was shown. The cycle of life is mysterious and plays out in incredible ways.

Specifically from the story of King David and Mephibosheth, we learn the following lessons on the principle of reciprocity:

1. **Reciprocity portrays us as truly godly people.** In ancient times, when a new king ascended to the throne, it was customary to eliminate any potential threats by eradicating the descendants of the previous king's family. However, David, in contrast to this norm, chose to be different and godly. Not minding all the evils that Saul did to him, he still resolved to show kindness to any of his remaining descendants.

2. **Reciprocity portrays us as faithful people**. Before Jonathan's death, he and David had made a covenant of friendship and loyalty. After Jonathan's death, David continued to honor this covenant. He understood the importance of keeping his promises and treating others with fairness and justice.

3. **True reciprocity is non-discriminatory**. Despite Mephibosheth's background, disability, and lower social status, Kind David's commitment to kindness and reciprocity made him elevate the disabled person to the level of an adopted son. This challenges us to show kindness to others, regardless of their race, ethnicity, gender, religion, social status, or economic background.

KEY TAKEAWAY

Devote yourself to acts of kindness; the world is already saturated with evil. Remember to look out for those in need and those who have been of help to you. They may not be asking, but reach out to them. Since it is absolutely true that we reap what we sow, then sow acts of kindness, love, forgiveness, encouragement, wise advice, feeding the poor, clothing the naked, referring people to jobs, supporting the needy and the helpless. Kindness opens life's doors.

PERSONAL REVIEW

1. Do you keep a record of your benefactors and reach out to them in gratitude?
2. How much are you devoted to non-discriminatory acts of kindness?
3. How faithful are you to your promises?

Respect Is Magnetic

> "Respect is one of the greatest
> expressions of love."
> **Don Miguel Ruiz**

Respect is a feeling of deep admiration for the qualities of someone or something. Many of our choices and desires in life are based on some form of respect. In other words, you can hardly choose to go after something or somebody without being driven by admiration.

The point here is: If you respect or admire it, your life will tilt in its direction, and you will have it. Jesus had an encounter with two personalities, Mary and Martha, in the biblical book of Luke, and He seized the opportunity to reveal the most essential truths about the principle of respect (Luke 10:38-42).

STORY BACKGROUND

Jesus had visited the house of Martha, who also had her sister, Mary, living with her. With Master Jesus visiting, it should have been obvious that his goal was not feasting and merry-making but ministering the Word of life and healing the sick. However, Martha preoccupied herself with elaborate preparation for refreshments while Mary sat to hear Jesus teach.

Martha burdened with much work, spoke up about Mary not helping prepare the refreshments. But Jesus replied that the Word is more important than the feast and that Mary's respect for it had made her esteem it above everything else. What the Word brings is eternal, and because she respects it, the rewards will never elude her.

WISDOM NUGGETS

Once your choice in life is clear, have respect for it. What you respect, you focus on becoming. What or who you respect will shape you. Take an admired mentor, for instance. You will realize that as you continually study or listen to them, you learn their choice of words (diction), mannerisms, work ethics, dress sense, and sometimes, ideologies. A similar thing happens in a marriage relationship where both partners understand the place of respect, irrespective of their differences. The harmony is often incredible.

There is more to learn about this principle from Mary and Martha's encounter with Jesus. Let us consider these lessons:

1. **Respect and associate with who or what will add value to your life**. Because Mary admired Jesus, she developed a teachable spirit towards Him. She sat at His feet, listened to Him, and waited for Him to teach her. Jesus praised her for choosing the best thing that would forever add value to her life.

2. **True respect ignores barriers.** Mary's respect for Jesus and His words made her overlook the barrier of gender relations. Even though it was unusual for a rabbi to teach women, she went for what she wanted anyway.

3. **True respect ignores opposition**. Despite the criticisms of her sister, Mary was neither deterred nor distracted. She kept her focus on Jesus and left Him to defend her.

KEY TAKEAWAY

Admiration is an infiltrating feeling; it allows access to what you respect. That was what Jesus was showing Martha as a principle. If you respect what can set you back, you will be hindered. Similarly, if you admire what advances you, you will tilt towards advancement. So be careful what you respect. One writer says, "You can't attract what you attack."

PERSONAL REVIEW

1. Which individuals do you admire the most in your life?
2. What specific values are the listed individuals adding to your life?
3. What conscious efforts are you making to benefit from these sources of value continually?

The 1 Kings Principle

Peace Propels Productivity

> "Peace is not merely a distant goal that we seek,
> but a means by which we arrive at that goal."
> — **Martin Luther King Jr.**

Peace refers to a state of tranquility or freedom from disturbances. The one undeniable condition under which time allows for anything to be built and progress achieved unhindered is in tranquility. The principle of peace is premised on the idea projected by God Himself, as revealed in the scriptures. Proverbs 16:7 says, "When a man's ways please the LORD, He makes even his enemies to be at peace with him" (NKJV). Romans 12:18 adds, "If it is possible, as much as depends on you, live peaceably with all men" (Romans 12:18, NKJV).

King David reigned 40 years over Israel and Hebron. History has it that he fought about nine wars during his reign as king. That was a lot of trouble for a man who had the desire to build God a house. So, he could not achieve that feat. However, the biblical book of 1 Kings has it that Solomon, his son, had peace all around him during his reign, which enabled him to build God the house (1 Kings 5:1-18; 6:1-37). Herein lies the power of this principle.

STORY BACKGROUND

In the early years of his reign as king, Solomon resolved to build the house of God that David, his Father, could not build due to the numerous wars he fought. David first conceived the vision, but the absence of peace robbed him of the proper atmosphere to achieve it.

So, King Solomon, being blessed with rest, as God had promised him, sent a message to the Sidonian king, Hiram, to assist him with wood supplies to enable him to build the house for God. Hiram, a long-standing friend of King David, obliged him. The two of them made a pact, and God gave them peace.

WISDOM NUGGETS

Peace is undoubtedly the scarcest resource in the world today. Nations, communities, and families around the world desperately crave it. The current situation of nations like Syria, Ukraine, and Palestine (Gaza) is a clear example of what the absence of peace can cause, with their previously famed beauty severely diminished. Of course, this also applies to many other nations that wars have ravaged in recent times. Even in nations that are plagued by internal communal clashes, the pace of progress has been extremely slow.

How about families? Many have become a shadow of their early years of bliss, with spousal differences tearing homes apart and leaving children in the loop.

What do we learn from all of this? The answers lie in the success that Solomon recorded:

1. **Without consciously fostering an atmosphere of peace, progress will be elusive.** The essence of peace in the building and development of any structure cannot be overemphasized. From our story background and introduction, it is clear that the principle of peace is a prerequisite for any form of progress to be attained or sustained. Nothing is built in a state of chaos and commotion. Clearly, King David could not build whatever God was going to be associated with in war.

   The same is true of life today. Political leaders roll out manifestos and promises during elections that end up not seeing daylight due to a waste of time-fighting critics and opposition parties, leaving their countries at waste. Families start out sharing dreams about a great future ahead to achieve, but spouses end up battling their differences and incompatibilities till everything that once was a beauty is torn to shreds.

   Peace was the key to King Solomon's success. It was the plan of God that he would achieve that feat only in a condition of tranquility. God shows us principles for achieving anything we wish through stories and events recorded in His Word. They are not just mere stories or events. We must take care to examine and apply them as shown. You cannot build successful dreams in a chaotic marriage. You cannot advance a nation while fighting wars. Suppose we can ensure a peaceful existence, whether in our homes, organizations, or nations. In that case, there is never a limit to the progress that we will achieve.

2. **Peace ensures a smooth flow of productivity and creativity**. Developmental ideas are much better generated and executed in an atmosphere of peace. The atmosphere of peace helped Solomon's workers to focus on their work without distractions or disruptions that could hinder their progress, and they could work without any fear or anxiety. Besides, the workers were free to explore new ideas and solutions without any pressure or fear of failure, which helped to push the boundaries of what was possible. The ultimate result was the masterpiece of a temple that they produced.

3. **Peace is very much achievable.** This is absolutely true. The pursuit of self-interest, instead of collective gains, is often the primary bane of peace. When we plan together and labor together but eye the gains covetously and greedily, then the access point for chaos is opened, and peace is immediately threatened. The desire for selfish gains in a collective venture must be tamed. The bond of peace is more important than any share of gain. Indeed, the true gain in any venture is the continued reign of peace after the whole bargain.

KEY TAKEAWAY

Every relationship (family, communal, national, or international) can thrive and survive if the pursuit of selfish gain is checked. According to the divine principle of peace, for us to succeed individually and collectively, we must keep our choices simple enough to gain and thrive with them.

PERSONAL REVIEW

1. What is the most important lesson you have learned from this principle of peace?
2. In what ways can you nurture a peaceful atmosphere in your home and other environments?
3. How will you personally prevent your personal interests from hindering the collective good?

The Daniel Principle

Courage Is the Bedrock of Conquests

"Courage is not simply one of the virtues,
but the form of every virtue at the testing point."
- C.S. Lewis.

C ourage is a rare virtue to possess. It is not just boldness; the doggedness is deeper. Its presence is best determined when there is a cause for fear, pain, or grief. In other words, strength in the face of fear, pain, or grief — this is courage. The ability to do what is right despite being frightened — this is courage. As Oswald Sanders says, "Courage is that quality of mind which enables people to encounter danger or difficulty firmly, without fear or discouragement."

Courage involves a willingness to persevere and withstand danger despite being fully aware of the cost of the resolve. The biblical book of Daniel, especially the story of the three Jews — Shadrach, Meshach, and Abednego - brings home the focus of the principle in this chapter.

STORY BACKGROUND

Daniel had been elevated as prime minister in the Babylonian Empire after he had told the king's dream and the interpretation. Daniel also helped in elevating the three Jews - Shadrach, Meshach, and Abednego - within the Babylonian provinces (Daniel 2:46-49).

The king, Nebuchadnezzar, erected a new image in Babylon, commanding everyone to fall down and worship it at the prompting sounds of instruments and music. Then, accusations against Shadrach, Meshach, and Abednego came to the king, saying that they worshipped not his God (the image). The king summoned them, told them the penalty for disobeying (which was death by roasting in a fiery fire furnace), and instructed that instruments and music prompts be sounded for them to bow to the image in his presence (Daniel 3:1-15).

The three Jews' answer to the king, even in the face of death, was simple: "O Nebuchadnezzar, we do not need to defend ourselves before you. If we are thrown into the blazing furnace, the God whom we serve is able to save us. He will rescue us from your power, Your Majesty. But even if he doesn't, we want to make it clear to you, Your Majesty, that we will never serve your gods or worship the gold statue you have set up" (Daniel 3:16-18).

Then the king, in his rage, ordered that they be thrown alive and bound into the fiery furnace. But, it got interesting when the Almighty God, whom they served and courageously defended their faith in, was observed by the king to be moving about in the furnace of fire with them. And neither of them was burned. Even more astonishing was that the heat of the fire had been so much that the people who threw them into it had been killed instantly.

In that astonishment, the king ordered again that the three young men should walk out of the fire, which they did. He recognized and adored the Almighty God that the Jews served and trusted in. He also decreed that no one should bring any accusations against the God of the Jews anymore in Babylon. Then, he further promoted the three courageous men (Daniel 3:19-30).

WISDOM NUGGETS

Courageous people are not extra special beings. They are just as human as everyone else, except that they know what they believe and want, and they go after it. This is why the late Nelson Mandela said, "I learned that courage was not the absence of fear, but the triumph over it. The brave man is not he who does not feel afraid, but he who conquers that fear."

The amazing story of the three Jewish men underscores salient truths about the principle of courage:

1. **Success is on the other side of fear.** Fear is the greatest enemy of courage, and it is a common challenge to all humans. However, what sets us apart as courageous conquerors is our ability to face our fears and conquer them. As in our story background, every situation in Life presents us with the "bow before the image" demand and the "fiery furnace" penalty for daring to be different.

Yes, you will always be faced with fearful threats for daring not to be mediocre, for daring not to align with the status quo. You will be criticized or victimized for daring to do something great that nobody in your bloodline has ever dared or for daring to defend your faith at work bravely. However, if you choose not to "bow," your tests will eventually turn to testimonies.

2. **God is the surest anchor of courage**. Why do the courageous people who dare to take the unpopular route come off with extraordinary results? It is because they dare to trust that the "Fourth Man" will not let them down. They dare to believe that once they lose sight of the common shores, they may only discover new grounds. They dare to envision and believe that there is a brighter future to attain on the other side of every fiery furnace (fear).

3. **Courage is a journey, not a destination**. Do challenges ever end? No. They are meant to be conquered at every step of the journey of Life, but only by the brave. Way too many people remain unnecessarily single for fear of marriage. Too many people linger on meager salaries for fear of starting and failing on that business idea. Too many are trapped in mediocrity for fear of uncertainties. The faith leap of Life can only be taken by YOU! Get fired up and take that leap of Life today. Most of your fears are just a mirage. You launch out, get there, and realize they never existed. You discover that they were just scarecrows to keep you ordinary and underachieving in Life.

When you dare to stir courage into being, fear dreads you. There are numerous advantages you arouse into action for your benefit when you wake up and exude courage in your Life's pursuits. Success can smell courage and never refuses her wooing. In fact, they travel in the same direction and accompany each other anytime, anywhere.

KEY TAKEAWAY

Courage is a must in this jungle called Life, and fear is a mirage and a big NO. Intimidate it and never mingle with it. Continue to confront and conquer your fear because you are meant to be a victor, not a victim.

In addition:

- If you are timid, take some classes to help you.
- If you are shy, seek some help.
- If you have a phobia that suppresses your confidence, get some help.
- If you are a loner, loosen up and mingle, but do so rightly.
- Socialize but only make friends that spur you and motivate you to great and resourceful feats.
- Get mentors - those who know how to get things done.
- If you have given up on a dream because you tried and failed, dare to dream anew—fellowship with dream achievers. Be humble, ask questions, and be open to learning.

PERSONAL REVIEW

1. What is your understanding of the principle of courage?
2. In what areas of your Life do you need to apply this principle more than before?
3. Is there any vision you have failed to implement or stopped implementing halfway because of fear? What new resolution are you making concerning this vision?

The Matthew Principle

Profit Is a Mandate

> "Profit is like oxygen, food, water, and blood for
> the body; they are not the point of life,
> but without them, there is no life."
> **- James C. Collins.**

Profit is gain, whether it is financial or otherwise. It is the difference between the amount earned and the amount invested in buying, operating, or producing something. Slothfulness is the most repulsive thing in any venture, as it guarantees that the whole essence of the venture is a waste of time and resources.

Profit is the reason for all dealings in whatever sphere of engagement. If something is not envisioned for progress, growth, multiplication, and profit, then its existence should be questioned.

However, we must not be oblivious to the temptation to pursue dishonest and destructive gain by any means possible. So, the question is, how should we profit? The Parable of the Talents in the biblical book of Matthew, as told by Jesus Christ, clarifies that the principle of profit is hinged on rightful investments and trading of our talents.

Talents, here, represent our comparative abilities and possessions (money, skills, time, knowledge, etc.).

STORY BACKGROUND

In the Parable of the Talents, Jesus likens the Kingdom of Heaven to a master who committed investable talents (abilities) to his three servants as he embarked on a long trip. They were expected to give an account of their endowments on his return.

One servant received five talents, another three talents, and the last, one talent. Both servants that had the five and the two talents, respectively, engaged their talents for profit (faithfully) and gained double their initial investments. The last servant, however, got lazy with his one talent. He neither invested in it nor engaged in any form of trade that could have resulted in gain. Instead, he kept it just as received, to be given back to his master on his return.

Soon, their master returned and called them to account for the talents received. The servants with the five and the two talents received a commendation for their sense of investment and profitability. The servant with the one talent, however, received condemnation. The master scolded his slothfulness and inability to maximize his talent, even in the smallest form. Simply put, the slothful servant had failed in the principle of profit (Matthew 25:14-30).

WISDOM NUGGETS

The principle of profit is captured in the scolding of the slothful servant, as recorded in Matthew 25:26-27: *"His lord answered and said unto him, Thou wicked and slothful servant, thou knewest that I reap where I sowed not, and gather where I have not strawed: Thou oughtest therefore to have put my money to the exchangers, and then at my coming I should have received mine own with usury"* (KJV).

The master's reference to "usury" is not an endorsement for exploiting people to gain profit by all means. It is to drive home the point that every talent is for profit and that rightful investment or trade is the key. That was why he said he could have received his own with usury (gain).

Here are further revelations about the principle of profit from the Parable of the Talents:

1. **Faithfulness is closely linked to profiting**. Notice that the servants were being rewarded for their faithfulness, but their faithfulness was measured based on profit. Profit here is synonymous with progress, growth, multiplication, improvement, self-development, proper character enhancement, good time management habits, overcoming bad habits, gaining financial prudence to get out of debt, becoming more responsible, and soaring above all forms of slothfulness.

   Whatever you do, remember that faithfulness must be the motive for your quest and craving for profit. God will never approve of profit made from exploitation. The principle of profit, as initiated by God, is a seed sown into good soil, and it will ultimately yield. Good and right trading (engaging and investing our time, abilities, knowledge, and resources) is naturally wired to yield us profit.

2. **God looks forward to the profits we make with our lives**. This is so because He equipped and empowered us to profit. As Deuteronomy 8:18 says, "Remember the LORD your God. He is the One who gives you the power to be successful." Isaiah 48:17 also says, "Thus says the LORD, your Redeemer, the Holy One of Israel; I am the LORD your God who teaches you to profit, who leads you by the way that you should go" (NKJV).

3. **Shun laziness to fulfill the profit mandate**. Do not be lazy in living. Investment is not all about money and multiplying it in stocks and properties (real estate). Time is one of the greatest resources we have to invest rightly for profit. When parents neglect to invest time in their children for proper upbringing, they struggle and cry over their delinquencies in their adult years. When a student fails to invest time in his studies, the struggles wait at the door of opportunities requiring good qualifications in the future. When an artisan fails to invest time to learn and integrate the latest trends and innovations within his craft, he gets lost in the competition with his outdated craft skills.

KEY TAKEAWAY

Every profit requires work. So, update your knowledge and skills and evolve with the trends in your craft, business, industry, family structure, society, and the world at large. There must be no loose time; keep evolving and intentionally improving for consistent positive results.

Also, bear in mind that no quest or craving for profit must usurp another's advantage to survive or win. Nobody has to go down for you to win. Life is big enough for everyone to profit. Your profit will only count faithful to God if you gain it genuinely and righteously.

PERSONAL REVIEW

1. What have you personally learned from the Parable of the Talents?
2. Have you been profiting with your God-given talents and privileges?
3. What kind of profit are you making — godly or ungodly?

The Isaiah Principle

Calmness Is the Cure for Crisis

> "By staying calm, you increase your resistance against any kind of storm."
> — **Mehmet Murat ildan**

One thing that will never cease in Life is threatening situations. Trouble is a constant occurrence, except that it will keep resurfacing in different forms. At such moments, what attitude or approach do you quickly resort to - calmness or agitation?

Calmness is a state or quality of being free of agitation or strong emotions. However, as we will see shortly, this is not mere quietness or folding of the arms, doing nothing. This principle is well-portrayed in the story of King Hezekiah of Judah in the biblical book of Isaiah. Interestingly, several other references in the Bible also show calmness as God's accepted attitude toward any threatening situation we encounter.

Here are some examples:

"Be still, and know that I am God; I will be exalted among the nations, I will be exalted in the earth!" (Psalms 46:10).

"And Moses said to the people, "Do not be afraid. Stand still and see the salvation of the LORD, which He will accomplish for you today. For the Egyptians whom you see today, you shall see again no more forever. The LORD will fight for you, and you shall hold your peace." (Exodus 14:13-14).

In case your first resort during Life's storm is agitation, those are God's recommendations to you. What you are doing is being agitated, which is the exact opposite, and it is a clear expression of your lack of confidence in divine help.

STORY BACKGROUND

Sennacherib, king of Assyria, acclaimed to be the most powerful king on the earth at the time, had besieged Judah. He sought to conquer Judah as he had done to other powerful nations. So, he sent a messenger to proclaim his besiegement and threatened Judah to surrender at will to avoid the gruesome war.

Sennacherib's messenger, Rabshakeh, did justice to his assignment of driving home to Judah the fear and dread of his master, who truly had conquered greater nations than Judah in terms of military strength. He haughtily mocked that if the gods of those defeated great nations could not deliver them from King Sennacherib, then Jehovah, the Almighty God whom Judah served, would not be able to deliver Judah either.

When the news came to Hezekiah, king of Judah, he and his men tore their clothes. Covered in sackcloth, they sought the Prophet Isaiah. Trouble like none other had fallen upon Judah, and they sought the Lord's help. God's simple reply to King Hezekiah through Prophet Isaiah was:

*"And Isaiah said unto them, Thus shall you say unto your master; thus saith the LORD, **Be not afraid** of the words that you have heard, wherewith the servants of the king of Assyria have blasphemed me."* (Isaiah 37:6, KJV)

Since Sennacherib's boast was against the Almighty God whom Judah served, He took up the challenge by sending an angel who went through the Assyrian army camp that night. And by morning, 185,000 warriors had died. Then, the great Sennacherib was swallowed up in confusion and returned home - not just defeated but disgraced. And years later, he was killed by his sons in his shrine (Isaiah 36:1-22; 37:1-38).

WISDOM NUGGETS

Staying calm in the face of raging situations is a solid attraction point for divine help. Agitations or raging emotions never achieve the same result. Apparently, the reason God asks us not to be afraid or agitated in Life's challenges is that agitation is never wired as a solution to anything. It is, in fact, a total waste of time and effort.

But will there ever come a time when we will not have a situation that excites agitation? No, except in death. So, how do we put anxiety under control? Here are clues from the victory of Judah over Sennacherib:

1. **Understand that challenges do not last forever**. Look back on your Life, at least to the extent you can recall, understanding that a given situation was trouble, either for you personally or for your family. If this was 20 years ago, is it still there now? If not, how long did it last? Maybe weeks or months, or a year or more? Can you recall the many troubles that have come and gone? And so many more in recent times that you had come through?

    Many troubles come and go. Somehow, you get around them. They may have cost you much, but you got around them. The positive mental consciousness that troubles come and go is a good place to start. Believe and declare continuously that "this too will pass."

2. **Understand that agitation and anxiety solve no problem.** Taking to agitation is like being under the shower with soap lather washing down over you, and because some of the lather gets into your eyes, you decide to turn off the shower and start screaming for help. Here is what settling for anxiety does to you during a crisis:

    -   It blurs your reasoning. You stop thinking, at least, constructively.
    -   It distracts your abilities.
    -   It weakens you.

- It endangers your health in many ways.
- It empowers the situation.
- It lengthens the existing time of the situation.
- It gives you a sense of failure.
- It makes you hateful.
- It makes you objectionable to others since you are always reactive.
- It weakens your confidence.
- It enslaves your mind.
- It magnifies a simple problem.
- It steals your rest and sleep.
- It makes you mentally unfit.

Anxiety does a lot of costly harm to its host. The most harmful thing is that it does nothing to change the situation. So, the troubles remain while you are losing every other thing that is of value to you.

3. Calmness equips you for victory over storms.

Here is what employing calmness does to you during a crisis:

- It keeps you stable — mentally, physically, and spiritually.
- It allows you to see clearly and understand the situation at hand.
- Your reasoning is intact while you engage in thinking about what to do.
- If you need to call someone, ask for information, or do something to initiate the first right step toward a solution, you are stable enough to figure that out.

- Your confidence stays intact.
- It keeps your blood pressure normal.
- Your mind is alert.
- The problem remains just what it is. No magnifier.
- It is just a situation that needs fixing, whether you know how to or not. So you do not feel like a failure.
- No health threat.
- If it is beyond natural fixing, you can confidently trust and pray.

KEY TAKEAWAY

Those who know the art of calmness in crisis often seem supernatural to those who feel every crisis means the world is caving in over them. Note again that calmness is not in any way indolence. It is not a carefree attitude or a display of laziness or even fright or fear — chickening out. No. Calmness is a great skill. When you go quietly on the outside, you see more clearly from the inside, and when you move with action, the target is precise. And when you know exactly what to do about anything, precision becomes your strength.

PERSONAL REVIEW

1. How do you handle crisis situations?
2. How do you plan to apply this principle of calmness to your Life?
3. Why is it unreasonable and unhealthy to resort to anxiety and agitation in a crisis?

The John Principle

Connection Is the
New Currency

> "Connection is the heart of the human experience.
> It is what makes Life worth living."
> **- Janine Garner.**

These days, it is very common to hear that your network is your net worth. There are kernels of truth in this. Connection is the point at which two or more things are joined, attached, or united. This explains the interrelationships that exist among human beings, and it illustrates the principle of connection, as drawn from the teaching of Jesus Christ in the biblical book of John (John 15:1-17).

Today, the power of the principle of connection is undeniable before our eyes. It now matters so much to what circle you belong to, who you know, and the groups or institutions you are affiliated with. While the principle of connection has existed for centuries, the fact remains that today, across all spheres of Life, almost nothing moves for anyone without affiliate connections.

The reality is that the world is now more segmented into all strata — academic, business, social, religion, communities, politics, etc. Humans are now confined and boxed into finding meaning for their existence and success only within affiliate connections. However, when Jesus taught this principle in the Gospel of John, it was a pointer to connecting to Him (the Life), as we can only find purpose and success by connecting to the right source (the Vine).

SUBJECT BACKGROUND

Jesus draws the illustration (parable) of the Husbandman (the Father), the Vine (Jesus Himself), and the branches (believers). He describes God as the owner who tends the vineyard, and he describes Himself as the Vine (trunk) on which every branch is grafted. Of course, we know that no branch exists on its own except attached to the trunk.

The trunk bears the root (bottom) and all other parts of the tree (top). It is the source and supplier of the nutrients that sustain the branches, the leaves, and, ultimately, the fruits.

He says in John 15:4-5: "Abide in Me, and I in you. As the branch cannot bear fruit of itself, except it abide in the Vine; no more can you, except you abide in Me. I am the Vine; you are the branches: he who abides in Me, and I in him, the same brings forth much fruit: for without Me you can do nothing" (NKJV).

Christ observes that if a branch fails to connect and, therefore, lacks the nutrients to stay alive and connected to the Vine, it is cut off and turns to waste. "If a man abides not in Me, he is cast forth as a branch, and is withered; and men gather them, and cast them into the fire, and they are burned" (verse 6).

The whole essence of connection is to keep alive, within your natural habitat and purpose, and ultimately bear fruits. God made it so, and His pleasure is in our fruitfulness. "Herein is My Father Glorified, that you bear much fruit; so shall you be My Disciples" (verse 8).

The agricultural metaphor used by Jesus in his teaching simplifies this principle. We can apply this principle to all other walks of Life and see that it is true. Nothing fails on purpose if it is rightly engrafted within its natural place or affiliation. The right connection is the key to every success.

WISDOM NUGGETS

The agricultural procedure of engrafting is a true lesson for Life. The connection can be positive or negative. Many are wrongly engrafted and seek success where it cannot be found. Imagine that you take a tomato branch and engraft it into a coconut trunk. What happens? You guessed right — it will die with no fruit or success. Thus, the principle of connection, as taught by Christ, emphasizes the following:

1. **Right connections determine the right results**. Our affiliations determine a lot for us in our world today. However, as we seek those connections amidst the quest to succeed, we must be careful to be engrafted within our true

117

source. Connect with your own kind of purpose rightly. Do not keep a wrong circle and expect fruits it cannot bear.

If your chances in Life are as good as your affiliations, then it is time to assess and review your associations. Affiliate groups and connections are so important, as you will always produce after the underlying philosophy. If you ever have questions about the trajectory of your progress in Life, check your affiliations and connections.

2. **Be intentional with your connections.** The connection must be an intentional decision for you; very intentional. Treat it as a matter of Life and death because most of your connections will eventually determine Life or death for you.

Make connections in relation to your dreams and purpose. "Like pairs attract," as they say. "Birds of a feather flock together". Even the Bible says, *"Deep calls unto deep"* — (Psalms 42:7). People go down or rise due to the affiliations they are invested in. Many connect just for social status. This should not be. Connect for "dreams status," "purpose status," and "success status."

Again, if your connections are not bringing success — that is, if you cannot measure your fruitfulness, it is time to review them.

3. **Ditching wrong connections does not include the marital relationship.** Here is a word of caution. Do not view or interpret this principle of connection and compatibility as a reason to ditch your marriage. The

principle has nothing to do with marital incompatibilities. The principle Jesus taught, using the illustration of the "Vine and Branches," says nothing about marriage since neither spouse is a vine or a branch.

KEY TAKEAWAY

Jesus taught that fulfilling purpose and becoming successful in Life can only be achieved by getting the required nutrients from your actual source. This principle is true for every right connection and affiliation. Again, be very intentional about your association and connections — it is your number one responsibility in Life.

PERSONAL REVIEW

1. Are you engrafted rightly or wrongly? Do you need to be more informed or stronger when engaging in any connection?
2. Are your present connections meeting your aspirations? Are they spurring you towards success and fulfillment?
3. What measures will you take henceforth to disengage from wrong connections?

The Philippians Principle

Humility Is the Passcode for Exaltation

> "Humility is nothing else but a right judgment of ourselves."
> **— William Law.**

Humility is humbleness in character and behavior. The Apostle Paul, in his letter to the Philippian Church, describes humility as a mindset that can be imbibed.

Humility is one virtue that, no matter how highly placed or privileged you are, will portray you as being less of your actual status — while actually helping to safeguard your status and positioning you for greater heights!

The opposite of humility is pride — an unreasonable overestimation of one's importance.

Apostle Paul uses Christ, the perfect exemplar of this principle, to admonish that anyone who wants to follow this route to exaltation similarly must imbibe His mindset. So, this principle is premised on selflessness.

SUBJECT BACKGROUND

Apostle Paul, in correcting clique forming and status struggles, admonished the believers in Philippi: "Let nothing be done through strife or vainglory (forming sides), but in lowliness of mind let each esteem other better than themselves. Look not every man on his own things, but every man also on the things of others" (Philippians 2:3-4).

Then he presents the mindset of Christ as the perfect remedy, adding that it can be imbibed: "Let this mind be in you, which was also in Christ Jesus..." (Philippians 2:5).

Jesus Christ came to the earth as God the Son. Yet, He stripped Himself of that Divine status, suspended His rights of Deity, and humbled Himself. He took the form of a servant in the likeness of men and died on the cross to save us from our sins (Philippians 2:6-8).

The apostle further revealed that the outright reward for such a wondrous act of humility was exaltation, making all powers subject to His exalted Name, whether in heaven, on earth, or under the earth. Jesus Christ is Lord! (Philippians 2:9-11).

WISDOM NUGGETS

Humility is not in mere words but in acts. Anyone can fake the words of Jesus Christ, but no one can fake the example of His humility. Even if you try, you cannot sustain it through time because Life will test your ego. Imagine God living amongst men in such a humble way as to become the perfect example and yardstick for measuring humility till eternity.

If we attempt to juxtapose that with the realities of our world, we might be arousing buried emotions. Who remembers that supervisor at work? He was not the Manager, the Director, or the CEO. Still, he could not help bullying and disdaining others while bragging about his status (not that bullying would be right if he occupied a higher position, anyway). Bet you can recall the Assistant Professor who acted like he owned the school, terrorizing students in class?

Everyone tends to go heady as the achievements come rolling in, as the echelon rises, and as the finances boom. But Jesus has shown us how this can be avoided through the following tenets of the principle of humility:

1. **Humility must be consciously cultivated**. Humility is the stabilizer that must be intentionally activated; otherwise, the oppressor personality will set in, and pride will take hold. It is said of Jesus Christ that He personally "took the form of a servant." Naturally, with every achievement comes some measure of ego; however, ego must be tamed. Positions are for bettering people, systems, processes, structures,

institutions, society, etc. The ego is the only thing that distracts and alters this view.

Oppressive tendencies rise from the ego; they destroy people, systems, institutions, and society. There is no humility in oppressors, only pride. And no proud person has ever made an all-round success of any system or society. Pride precedes a fall.

2. **Humility is fueled by selflessness.** Self-centeredness is the root of all pride. Humility is selfless, which is why it easily leads to exaltation. Power is for advancing people. No selfish person deserves exaltation, according to God's principle. Use every exalted position to advance people and the purpose of God. If you are a father, husband, Manager, supervisor, pastor, leader, legislator, governor, president, or whatever. You are naturally a prone victim of ego and pride. But this principle is for you; humility will save you from those. Christ's humility brought salvation to humanity (those who believe and everyone can believe).

3. **Humility is about the common good**. Humble people seek a common goal and usurp nobody. They understand the win-win principle and never assume that the world revolves around them alone. Humble people do not care who gets the glory but that the goal is achieved and the team wins. They make sacrifices. They are not vengeful and do not seek others' hurt. They tolerate love, are supportive, and are persevering.

KEY TAKEAWAY

Humility is not stupidity but an intentional decision to be different and lead from the standpoint of right conduct that enhances everyone; it is about win-win. Using your power and position to advance people's lives and improve society when threat and oppression are the general trend is humility. Jesus could have punished sinners, but He chose to die for them instead. Every act of humility ends in exaltation of some sort. Even if it is not a physical elevation to an office or position, it does end in exaltation that becomes a reference for others to imbibe.

PERSONAL REVIEW

1. What important lessons have you learned from this principle of humility?
2. In what ways are you exercising your power and authority?
3. What conscious efforts will you be making henceforth to practice Christ-like humility?

The Nehemiah Principle

Availability Supersedes Ability

> "God does not begin by asking our ability, only our availability, and if we prove our dependability, He will increase our capability."
> **- Neal A. Maxwell.**

In most situations of Life, there is often much emphasis on ability. However, ability without availability becomes more or less a liability. Whereas, even without the required level of ability, individuals who are available and willing to learn and grow by putting in their time can still achieve tremendous success. This is the vital principle in the book of Nehemiah.

When the news of Jerusalem being in utter ruin got to Nehemiah, it disturbed his heart. He could not bear living with the reality that his fatherland was in shambles. He immediately swung into action, praying for God's mercy (Nehemiah 1:1-11; 2:1-11). He knew that the city would not rebuild itself; someone had to rise to the occasion. This is the principle of availability.

The principle of availability affirms that availing oneself to mobilize towards changing situations for the better is the bedrock of any accomplishment. The rebuilding of Jerusalem was certainly God's will, but someone had to be available for use. That was the opportunity that Nehemiah seized. The same is true of the projects and dreams around our lives.

STORY BACKGROUND

Nehemiah, the Jew, was King Artaxerxes' cupbearer in Shushan. News reached him by Hanani, another Jew, that the remnant of Jews after the captivity lived in grave suffering and reproach. Jerusalem, their homeland, had its wall broken down and the gates burnt and left in waste. Nehemiah cried and offered prayers to God on behalf of the Jews for divine mercy.

In his grief for Jerusalem, he was serving the king wine one day when the king noticed his countenance and asked what he could do to help relieve his worries. Nehemiah requested that the king grant him permission to return to his fatherland and rebuild the wall, which lay in ruin. God granted him a favor, as the king obliged, authorizing his mission with letters backing him to get supplies from governors to rebuild the broken wall and gates of Jerusalem.

Nehemiah did arrive in Jerusalem and mobilized the remnant of the Jews for the work. Although they faced great opposition and threats, they stood their ground against their enemies. Phase after phase, they progressed and achieved the rebuilding of the wall and gates of Jerusalem (Nehemiah 4:1-23; 6:15-16).

WISDOM NUGGETS

What comes first to mind in this subject of availability is presence. It is easy to assume that being present means being available. But this seems wrong. Presence does not necessarily translate to availability. To achieve tangible causes in Life, presence must go beyond being around. Availing oneself must be about accomplishing a purpose and standing tall against the odds that challenge the actualization of the goal. No goal is without an opposition or hurdle to cross.

Are you available? Take, for instance, the task of parenting; that a mother or a father is present does not guarantee a wholesome upbringing. Parenting is one of Life's toughest tasks. It is not to be done carelessly. It is always a challenging task for those who want to raise wholesome adults.

You may be the CEO of your business. You have won customers and clients who trust your goods and services. How available are you to the business and your customers? Bear in mind that your competitors (the opposition) are not folding their hands and allowing you a free cruise. How conversant are you with evolving trends, especially technology that is changing the face of business and deciding customers' satisfaction quest?

Are you job hunting or looking to take up a new but more fulfilling job role? How available are you with the requisite skills, knowledge, or information? Are you waiting for a new role with old skills and obsolete knowledge? Are you exploring the right or the wrong avenues for the opportunities you desire?

Here are crucial lessons to imbibe on availability from the story of Nehemiah and the rebuilding of Jerusalem.

1. **Availability requires purpose**. Nehemiah showed us that availability requires a clear purpose. He was dedicated to rebuilding the walls of Jerusalem, and nothing could dampen his spirit or distract him. He made himself available to God to take on this important task, and God used him to lead the way. The principle of availability shows us that availability is vision-oriented. An available person understands purpose and is willing to learn and be taught. He is growth-conscious and a team player.

2. **Availability requires a sense of leadership**. Availability bestows on you the responsibilities of leadership. It may not immediately be leading others; it may just be leading yourself first by taking responsibility. It involves identifying a need that will not change except when an external force acts, and you make yourself that required force. An available person is a potential leader. He stirs the force of change into action. God backs available people once there is a cause to accomplish. Whatever you desire to accomplish, be it a healthy marriage relationship, raising wholesome kids, growing a business, or achieving academic or career success, make yourself sincerely available and ready to work through the hurdles. You will surely see the force of grace backing your efforts.

3. Availability requires sacrifice. Availing yourself demands sacrifice. Nehemiah gave up his comfortable position to serve God's purpose, and he put in the necessary hard work to complete the project despite all the opposition. More often than not, championing a cause that holds benefits for people other than yourself will require you to suspend personal gains temporarily. Most leadership roles demand sacrifice across all fields. Many great inventions emerged this way.

KEY TAKEAWAY

If you make yourself available to God and humanity, you will do common things in an uncommon way and with uncommon results. Availability and not mere ability ensures accomplishments and success in any cause you desire.

PERSONAL REVIEW

1. Are you prioritizing ability above availability, or are you ensuring a healthy blend of both?
2. In what ways will you increase your availability for God and humanity?
3. What barriers will you need to remove to make yourself more available to your family and those who need you the most?

The Joshua Principle

Focus Is the Fulcrum of Purpose

> "Whenever you want to achieve something,
> keep your eyes open, concentrate, and make
> sure you know exactly what it is you want.
> No one can hit their target with their
> eyes closed."
> **- Paulo Coelho.**

Nothing keeps one on the course of purposeful achievements like focus. Anybody will fail on a mission, no matter how equipped or qualified, the moment he gives in to distractions and loses focus. Focus is the ability to pay attention and concentrate on a goal to see it through as desired or expected.

In a world with so many demands and expectations to meet (personal, family, communal, occupational, etc.), we are often saddled with many activities. However, the principle of focus remains the one timeless skill to develop for assured success in our aspirations.

God introduced Joshua to this principle as soon as he was saddled with the responsibility of leading the Israelites after Moses had passed on. God instructed Joshua in the biblical book named after him that success lies in maintaining good focus.

STORY BACKGROUND

After the death of Moses, God chose Joshua, the son of Nun, to lead the Israelites. God promised Joshua to be with him on the journey of leading Israel and would give him victory over his adversaries as He did with Moses, his predecessor. God, however, admonished him to be strong and courageous. God told him: "Only be thou strong and very courageous, that thou mayest observe to do according to all the law, which Moses my servant commanded thee: turn not from it to the right hand or to the left, that thou mayest prosper whithersoever thou goest." (Joshua 1:7).

Joshua's success was guaranteed if he kept focus on the Law of God. "Turn not from it to the right hand or to the left, that you may prosper whithersoever you go."

Again, He told him:

"This book of the law shall not depart out of thy mouth, but thou shalt meditate therein day and night, that thou mayest observe to do according to all that is written therein: for then thou shalt make thy way prosperous, and then thou shalt have good success" (Joshua 1:8).

God instructs that the principle of focus on the Law would entail "speaking," "meditating," and "doing." That way, Joshua would prosper and have good success. (Joshua 1:1-9).

WISDOM NUGGETS

This principle, as introduced by God, still holds true today in our quest to achieve our dreams and aspirations. The common bane to every dream and goal is distraction. Distraction sways focus to less important or completely meaningless activities. Every failure is an offshoot of a lost focus. That is why knowing your mission and prioritizing it helps you focus right.

More importantly, from the principle of focus, as laid down by God for Joshua, we learn the following pivotal truths:

1. **Focus requires active nurturing.** Why do many fail and only a few succeed? It is because the focus is costly and easy. It is a skill that must be learned and perfected. As God said to Joshua, nurturing focus is a daily task that would involve his utterances, his mind (an active spirit and mind through meditation), and his behavior. If a dream goal or aspiration is worth living for, then focus is worth all the training, practicing, and mastering that is required to make it a lifestyle.

2. **Focus shapes destiny.** Nothing will frame you positively or negatively like what you focus on. The truth about Life is that everyone is focused on something, and the outcome will eventually tell what it was. Why are people more likely to focus on things that are contrary to what they really want

to become in Life? It is because it is less tasking to dwell on distractions — all it takes is just to join the flow and cruise. But for those who have an uncommon purpose that transcends the status quo, they know they have to create the Life they wish for against the odds. That is a lifetime of work, happening daily as you sync your utterances, thoughts, conducts, movements, associations, and everything else. That is certainly a lot of work, but it is very much worth it.

3. **Focus puts you in control.** Focus will help you to conserve and channel your momentum for optimal efficiency in achieving your goals and aspirations. It will help you stay in control of your set cause. It is the antidote to distractions. In fact, focus is power. This is why you sooner or later gain mastery in whatever you choose to focus on.

KEY TAKEAWAY

Whatever you identify as being right for you — in alignment with your mission and purpose — focus on it. Channel your momentum and resources on your focus, avoiding all distractions. It is only a matter of time before you start to count your blessings and rake in the harvest. All great feats were built this way.

To improve your power of focus, do these:

- Prioritize whatever goals you set and desire to achieve.
- Identify the possible distractions from the beginning.
- Set a time within which you engage in the activities/tasks for the set goals.
- Intentionally avoid people, places, activities, acts, etc., that made your list of possible distractions.

- If certain things in your personality made your list of possible distractors, you need help with "you." Funny but true! So, find someone who understands your mission and nature and can be of help to you.
- For every dream or goal you seek to accomplish, be sincere. It is okay to find a temporary mentor, trainer, or guardian as you take on that set goal.
- Since success rests on how committed you are to focusing, endure the tough phases. Set your eyes on the envisioned accomplishment, which, more often than not, turns out greater than you ever dreamed.
- Build some resilience and tenacity.
- Have your superiors know about your quest; request that they observe you sincerely assess and appraise you after a while.
- Be conscious of your alertness and mental health. Do not kill relationships you may need by being too rigid in focusing on your cause. In other words, once in a while, loosen up and unwind. Exercise, read, take a vacation, and be whole!

PERSONAL REVIEW

1. Outline the key lessons you have learned from the principle of focus.
2. What constitutes the main barriers to your focus?
3. What steps will you be taking henceforth to conquer distractions and improve your focus?

About Olu Ojeikere

OLU OJEIKERE is a Teacher, Preacher, Motivational Speaker, and Licensed Social Worker. He is a firm believer that crises in life are not always resolved by strength but by wisdom and that where we are today and where we will be tomorrow will be determined by our level of wisdom.

He is one of the Ordained Resident Pastors in Abundant Life Christian Center Church in Brooklyn under the vibrant leadership of Drs. Festus and Anthonia Adeyeye.

Olu and his lovely wife, Edna, live in New York with their two children, Esther and Daniel.

For speaking engagement, counseling, and consultation: oluojeikere@yahoo.com, https://oluojeikere.com/

Also, By Olu Okeikere

Principles for a Year-Round Winning Life: 365 Daily Wisdom Nuggets

This book will provide you with God's scriptural wisdom and life applications to situations encountered every day. With this book in your hand and its words in your heart, your victory over the many challenges of Life is guaranteed.

9 781734 399189